A. A. Milne

By THOMAS BURNETT SWANN

Florida Atlantic University

Twayne Publishers, Inc.   ::   New York

CARNEGIE LIBRARY
'IVINGSTONE COLLEGE
..ISBURY N. C. 28144

Copyright © 1971 by Twayne Publishers, Inc.

All Rights Reserved

Library of Congress Catalog Card Number: 78–120527

MANUFACTURED IN THE UNITED STATES OF AMERICA

828.912
Sw972

To MARGARET HALEY CARPENTER
Poet, Biographer, and Inspiration

82570

Acknowledgments

I wish to acknowledge with gratitude my debt to the following publishers for permission to use materials under their copyright:

E. P. Dutton and Company for quotations from *When We Were Very Young*, *Now We Are Six*, *Winnie-the-Pooh*, and *The House at Pooh Corner*, as well as from *It's Too Late Now* (published in America as *The Autobiography of A. A. Milne*); and finally, for the photograph of A. A. Milne which appears on the dust jacket of this volume.

The New York Graphic Society for quotations from *Once on a Time*.

Preface

There are writers like John Donne who prosper, fall into neglect, and require the resurrecting studies of critics and biographers to restore them to their deserved eminence. A. A. (Alan Alexander) Milne is as yet not such a writer: he is handed from generation to generation like a beloved teddy bear, and his reputation—safeguarded by *Winnie-the-Pooh* and *The House at Pooh Corner* and a little less massively by *When We Were Very Young* and *Now We Are Six*—has survived his death to flourish in the 1960's. But books, like beautiful women, live by adulation. It is not enough to praise them, and, having praised to feel that their place is secure, their authors assured of immortality. Since memories are short and printed paper is not immortal, it is necessary to repeat our praises at frequent intervals and in resounding tones. For this reason, this study, critical, analytical, and sometimes simply appreciative, is overdue. It may be argued that Milne belongs to children who are not concerned with literary criticism, analysis, or even appreciation. But parents must buy his books and introduce them to their children, and parents do read studies.

Milne deserves to be studied for a second reason. As he never tired of protesting, he was much more than a children's author. His four famous juveniles, published in still proliferating combinations and editions, together with a fairy-tale novel and a collection of stories for the very young, are the merest fraction of a formidable output which also includes thirteen volumes or pamphlets of articles, sketches, and introductions; four collections of plays; twelve separately published plays; five adult novels; two collections of poetry and a long philosophical poem; three collections of short stories; an autobiography and an autobiographical pamphlet. It is time to reevaluate Milne as a writer for adults; to isolate and commend the quality concealed in the quantity. The quality more than justifies a reevaluation, but the quantity is oppressively burdensome at times.

It was Milne's misfortune, as a writer if not as a man, to lead a singularly uneventful life. When a child, he was slight of build and delicate of disposition: "It was true that I had blue eyes and long flaxen hair; true that there were the Little Lord Fauntleroy days, and that on occasion I wore a velvet suit and lace collar; true that my hair curled naturally on my shoulders, after it had spent the night in papers."[1] When a young man, he dedicated his leisure to cricket, croquet, lawn tennis, cards, dancing, and conversation. After his reluctant stint in the army during World War I, he deliberately confined his adventures to being a model husband, an affectionate father, and a successful writer. Even a trip to the zoo could lacerate his nerves and leave him shaken and breathless: "When my boy was six years old he took me into the Insect House at the Zoo, and at the sight of some of the monstrous inmates I had to leave his hand and hurry back into the fresh air."[2] Since his marriage was happy and his son did not often take him to the Insect House, and since his climb to success was swift and fairly painless, his writing at times is actionless to the point of tedium. Reading his blander works, one is almost tempted to wish him a mistress or at least a few fistfights, and Grahame Greene has accused him of being not a humorist but a "cheer leader in a great community laugh."[3]

Milne had the additional misfortune to enjoy unlimited time in which to exhaust his exquisite but limited gifts; to write too often about the same subjects; to attempt themes which required an urgency and a pungency for which his experience had not prepared him. Like an archaeologist, the critic must sift his work and separate the authentic gold, the enduring artifacts, from clods of refuse and rubble. The sifting is complicated by Milne's inability to resist evaluating his own work. In introductions and articles, he writes about his books with such disarming persuasion that we are tempted to take him at his own evaluation. What he tells us about himself is wonderfully revealing of his models, his methods, his theories of composition; but his judgments are often suspect. When he rates his plays as his highest achievement and brands his children's books as "trifles for the young," the critic must be on guard.

Milne was much too prolific to invite a chronological approach to his entire career. Such an order is bound to seem disordered if not chaotic, as the reader lurches from novel to play to poem in the space of the same year. Furthermore, there is little perceptible pattern in the whole of his half a century as a writer. Except that his first book was his poorest, and that his best books, for the most part, were written in the 1920's, his career does not show a consistent development or decline. For example, in the year between two of his finest books, *When We Were Very Young* (1924) and *Winnie-the-Pooh* (1926), *A Gallery of Children* intrudes like a pale white slug between two butterflies. The only sensible approach is, therefore, to treat him separately as essayist, dramatist, writer of juveniles, and novelist. Such a division is anything but artificial. In his own mind·and in the eyes of the public, he enjoyed these four careers, which overlapped and sometimes coincided but remained on the whole distinct, so that theater-goers who endured *Belinda* were often unaware that the author was. also contributing essays to *Punch;* parents who read to their children "James James Morrison Morrison Weatherby George Duprez" rarely suspected that the poet of childhood also wrote drawing-room comedies about bigamists and temptresses; and readers of the novel *Mr. Pim Passes By* did not always recognize it as an adaptation of a successful play. For the sake of convenience, it is possible to arrive at the following separate chronologies:

Essays: 1905 (*Lovers in London*) to 1952 (*Year In, Year Out*)
Plays: 1917 (*Wurzel-Flummery*) to 1951 (*Before the Flood*)
Juveniles: 1917 (*Once on a Time*) to 1928 (*The House at Pooh Corner*)
Novels: 1921 (*Mr. Pim Passes By*) to 1946 (*Chloe Marr*)

The study opens with "Of Punch and Pacifism," a chapter concerning the articles, sketches, and introductions which may be loosely designated as essays. Not only do Milne's essays include his first and last books and thus constitute his longest career, but they serve as an excellent introduction to the man and the writer since some of them are personal reminiscences and since some of them introduce his own books in other fields. The next two chapters, "Drawing Rooms and Dreams" and "The Falling Star," discuss his plays, which in number and sheer wordage, though certainly not in excellence, compose his weightiest career. Three chapters—"A House for Many Summers," "Whisper Who Dares," and "The Peerless Pooh"—concern his least weighty but most enduring accomplishment, the juveniles. Chapter 7, "From Mr. Pim to Chloe Marr," concerns his novels; and Chapter 8, "Bagatelles," considers the by-products of his more substantial works: the poems and short stories which are too scattered and incidental to represent a fifth career. Chapter 9, "Back to the Bear," closes the book with a summary of his severe limitations, and a wholehearted endorsement of his achievements, particularly as the creator of Winnie-the-Pooh. His autobiographical works, *It's Too Late Now* and *When I Was Very Young*, which do not justify a whole chapter, are used throughout the study to illuminate his more creative books.

The dates given in the text represent the first editions or the first performances of Milne's works. The dates in the Selected Bibliography, however, represent the latest or the best or sometimes the only available editions. In other words, the text is designed for the chronological convenience of the reader, while the Bibliography is designed for the reader who, having read about Milne, wishes to find his books in their most attractive and accessible form. When it comes to the Christopher Robin poems and the Pooh stories, several editions are listed in the Bibliography, since each is distinguished from the others not only by title but by introduction, illustrations, and arrangement.

There are few more oppressive tasks than collecting and reading the whole of A. A. Milne. In the first place, some of his books are so forgotten that they are only obtainable in obscure secondhand bookshops or in the catacombs of the British Museum; in the second place, to disinter them is not to confront Lazaruses, flushed with life, but zombies better left in their graves. On the other hand, children who can say "now we are six" without knowing Christopher Robin have missed an incomparable playmate; a childhood with Pooh is like a chocolate soda without a cherry; and those who have read the best of Milne are wrong to suppose that his almost-best is not also worth a visit. In short, the purpose of *A. A. Milne* is to reaffirm the liveliness of the four great juveniles and, by dint of some ruthless rejecting and selecting, to choose a handful of plays, novels, and essays worthy to keep them company as honorable attendants, if not quite equals.

THOMAS BURNETT SWANN

Florida Atlantic University

Contents

Chronology

1882   Alan Alexander Milne, born on January 18 in London; third and youngest son of John Vine Milne, master of Henley House, a private school for boys.

1893–   Attends Westminster School.
1900

1900–   Attends Cambridge; edits the school magazine, *The*
1903   *Granta;* graduates with an Honours Degree in Mathematics.

1903   Becomes a free-lance writer in London and makes his first sale, a burlesque of Sherlock Holmes accepted by *Vanity Fair,* for fifteen shillings.

1905   Publishes his first and worst book, *Lovers in London,* a collection of light sketches about a young Englishman and his American sweetheart.

1906   Becomes assistant editor of *Punch* and contributes a weekly essay.

1910   Publishes *The Day's Play,* his first collection of *Punch* essays; sends a copy to the dramatist James Barrie, beginning a lifelong friendship.

1913   Marries Dorothy de Selincourt, the "Daphne" to whom he dedicated several later books.

1914   Joins the army and becomes a signalling officer and then an instructor on the Isle of Wight.

1916   Serves in France but returns to England to recuperate from a fever.

1917   His first play, *Wurzel-Flummery,* is performed in London; *Once on a Time,* later classified as a juvenile, is published as a "fairy-tale for adults."

1918   Leaves the army and embarks on a long career as dramatist.

1920   *Mr. Pim Passes By,* his most famous play, triumphs on the London stage; his only child, Christopher Robin, is born in August.

1921   *The Red House Mystery* and an adaptation of *Mr. Pim Passes By* introduce him as a novelist.

1924   *When We Were Very Young* immortalizes Christopher Robin and launches Milne on his most successful career as a children's writer.

1926   *Winnie-the-Pooh* begins the phenomenal sales which will make it the best selling of all Milne's books.

1927   *Now We Are Six* answers the public clamor for further poems about Christopher Robin.

1928   *The House at Pooh Corner* continues the adventures of Pooh, Piglet, Owl, Eeyore, Kanga, Roo, and Rabbit, and introduces the bouncy Tigger.

1929   Loses his favorite brother, Kenneth, to whom he will later dedicate his autobiography; publishes two of his best plays, *The Ivory Door* and *Toad of Toad Hall*, the second an adaptation of Kenneth Grahame's *The Wind in the Willows*.

1934   Publishes a sincere but unconvincing plea for pacifism, *Peace with Honour*.

1940–   Answers and disavows *Peace with Honour* with two
1941   pamphlets, *War with Honour* and *War Aims Unlimited*, in which he calls for unconditional victory.

1948   Christopher Robin, a Royal Air Force pilot during the war, is married to Lesley Selincourt.

1951   Publishes his last play, *Before the Flood*; sends the stuffed originals of Pooh and his friends on a tour of American libraries and bookstores.

1952   Publishes his final book, *Year In, Year Out*, a collection of essays in many moods.

1956   His death is mourned throughout the world.

1960   *Winnie-the-Pooh* is translated into Latin by Alexander Leonard and becomes a publishing prodigy.

1963   Frederick C. Crews parodies modern criticism in *The Pooh Perplex*.

1966   Walt Disney releases *Winnie-the-Pooh and The Honey Tree*.

CHAPTER 1

Of **Punch** *and* *Pacifism*

MILNE once wrote of himself: "So, too, when I am told, as I so often am, that it is time I 'came to grips with real life'— preferably in a brothel or a Public Bar where life is notoriously more real than elsewhere, minds more complex, more imaginative, more articulate, souls nearer the stars—I realize sadly that, even if I made the excursion, I should bring back nothing but the same self to which objection had already been taken."[1] In truth, he had no wish to make the excursion; for he was eminently satisfied with his "same self," an English gentleman of letters whose life was agreeable if not exciting, and whose daydreams allowed him the freedom of enchanted forests and the company of talking bears without any need to confront the Heffalumps of the psyche. When Milne is at his best—as a novelist sharing the vagaries of Mr. Pim or solving the mystery in the Red House, as a fantasist whose animals are more engaging than people and to whom fairy-tale princesses seem as modern as suffragettes, as a formal or familiar essayist after World War I—his world is infinitely visitable, a welcome escape from the brothels and bars of Naturalist fiction.

But Milne in his early essays, the pieces which launched his first career, gives the unfortunate impression that he spends his days at golf and croquet, his nights at house parties, and that he writes between strokes or cocktails. He is less a humorist than a farceur; he is not so much nimble as he is trivial; his style had been called "feathery," but he accumulates feathers until they become as ponderous as an overstuffed mattress. One wishes for bars and brothels after reading such paragraphs as: "I wonder if I shall be in good form this week-end at cricket and tennis, and croquet and billiards, and all the other jolly games I mean to play. Look at those children trying to play cricket in that dirty back-yard. Poor little beggars! Fancy living in one of those horrible

squalid houses. But you cannot spoil today for me, little back-
yards."[2]

In part, Milne was not to blame for such effusions. He was
young, inexperienced, and unknown. The popular journals of the
day, recovering and recoiling from the solemnities of the Victorian era, demanded just such trivia from aspiring authors; and
Milne was determined, indeed compelled, not only to aspire but
to succeed. When he went to London in 1903, a young man of
twenty-one just down from Cambridge, his total assets consisted
of a 320-pound subsidy from his father. His first sale, a burlesque
of Sherlock Holmes, brought him fifteen shillings from *Vanity
Fair*. At the end of three months, he had earned exactly five
pounds. At the end of the year, he had earned twenty pounds, of
which sixteen shillings and sixpence represented his first check
from *Punch*.

In his second year, however, he perfected a form of essay
which he called a "light article" and began to appear regularly in
such periodicals as *The Evening News, The Saint James' Gazette,
The Westminster Gazette*, and *Punch;* and by 1906 his formula
had earned him the position of assistant editor of *Punch*, with the
added and lucrative assignment of contributing one article a week
to the magazine. It is not surprising that he hesitated to depart
from the formula, even though his editor-in-chief, Owen Seaman,
recognizing his intelligence and education, urged him to write for
the serious reviews, since, as Milne himself admitted, "there was
nothing in any of my cricket sketches to indicate that I could even
work out a bowling analysis. . . . Could I not . . . show that
beneath the mask of levity there dwelt a serious purpose . . . ?"
But Milne insisted that "levity was no mask put on for the occasion. The world was not then the damnable world it is today; it
was a world in which imaginative youth could be happy without
feeling ashamed of its happiness. I was very young, very light-
hearted, confident of myself, confident of the future. I loved my
work; I loved not working; I loved the long week-ends with the
delightful people of other people's delightful houses. I loved being in love, and being out of love and free again to fall in love."[3]

Then, in late 1914, Milne went to war. The world he had loved,
it seemed, had not been childlike with youth but childish with
senility; and the writer of light articles, fighting in France, assumed a new seriousness both as a man and an artist. Even in his

callow days with *Punch,* his pieces had fitfully glowed with
warmth and charm: when he wrote about gardening; when he
wrote for the first and second times about golf and cricket.
In his postwar essays, the glow steadies into an almost constant flame.
He has learned the difference between the playful and the trivial;
that he can write formal essays as well as familiar; that it is not
always necessary to be amusing even when he is familiar: his
audience will not forsake him if he declares himself an ardent
pacifist and then, a few years later, endorses "war aims unlimited"
against Hitler, and still later approves the development of the
atom bomb.

Best of all, Milne became a literary critic whose outspokenness
is balanced by his love for tradition and whose opinions are so
artfully expressed that he is stimulating even when he is wrong.
No critic has surpassed his evaluations of Kenneth Grahame,
James Barrie, and Saki; and few critics in the age of Ezra Pound
and T. S. Eliot have equalled the boldness of such assertions as:
"The fact that in modern light verse the author does all the hard
work, and that in modern serious verse he leaves it all to the
reader, is a trade secret, unknown to a public which still supposes
that *Macbeth* is a 'bigger' performance than *A Midsummer
Night's Dream.*"[4]

Bad, better, or best, Milne's essays and sketches served the
commendable purpose of launching and helping to sustain him
as a writer. In the early pieces, successful with his readers but
shallow, contrived and dated, he at least became a stylist and
developed the flexibility which was destined to characterize his
plays, juveniles, and novels. In the later and stronger pieces, he
displays the mind, the manners, the tastes of a cultivated and
highly companionable author; and, a kind of Somerset Maugham
without cynicism, he shares his impressions with all the gracious-
ness of an accomplished host.

I   Lovers in London *and* Those Were the Days

Visitors to the British Museum who look under "Milne, A. A."
in the world's most monumental card catalogue will find a book
entitled *Lovers in London* (1905). Visitors to most other libraries,
British and American—even the Library of Congress—will look in
vain for the amorous and alliterative title. Its rarity is not an accident. *Lovers in London* is perhaps the silliest book ever to begin

a celebrated career. The twenty-four sketches which compose the collection and which first appeared in *The St. James' Gazette* concern the misadventures of an American girl and a young Englishman, who dance, play bridge, stroll in St. James' Park, visit a zoo, and become engaged. The girl is witless; the Englishman, who tells the story, is a would-be wit whose brightest sallies are typified by a comment he makes beside a cage in the zoo: "He is known as the Crab-eating Raccoon—no doubt because he eats crabs." Sold as a paperback for a shilling a copy, *Lovers in London* failed to recover the fifteen pounds which the publisher had advanced to Milne as royalties; and the best that reviewers—the few who noticed it—could find to say was that "the title anyhow was readable."[5] Milne agreed with the critics; and, when he had made his name with other books, he bought the copyright for five pounds to prevent a new edition.

In 1906 he began his weekly contributions to *Punch*, which continued to 1914 and, less frequently, from 1915 to 1920. The first of these essays and sketches, together with occasional verses, were collected into *The Day's Play* (1910), which Milne, doing his best to forget *Lovers in London*, insisted was his first *real* book. Later collections followed through the next eleven years in *The Holiday Round* (1912), *Once a Week* (1914), and *The Sunny Side* (1921); in 1929 the four volumes were combined into *Those Were the Days*. Milne half boasted and half confessed that the pieces represented an early style which he had since abandoned—a style which required that one "must be happy and careless, young and irresponsible." If, in his irresponsible period, he achieved no work of merit, "then this book shall be testimony of it. . . ."[6] His doubts were justified.

We have, for example, a dialogue between a young man who wishes to buy a present for his niece, Margery and the clerk:

"I want," I said, "a present for a child."

"Yes, sir. About how old?"

"It must be quite new," I said sternly. "Don't be silly, Oh, I see. Well, the child is only a baby."

"Ah, yes. Now here—if it's at all fond of animals—"

"I say, you musn't call it 'IT.' *I* get in an awful row if *I* do. Of course, I suppose it's all right for you, only—well, be careful, won't you?"[7]

After the waggish uncle has bought his niece a sideboard and a box of cigars, we are subjected to another vacuous interchange, this time of letters, and to several interminable conversations in which Margery speaks a nauseating form of babytalk: "at" for "that," "finking" for "thinking," and "bovver" for "bother." A similar series of sketches introduces a crowd of supercilious young people who call themselves the Rabbits and who spend their vacations engaging in conversation almost as asinine as that of Margery and her uncle—and less excusable. Milne's own experiences—a trip to Switzerland, a holiday in Cape Martin—often provided material for the Rabbits' adventures; and his own friends, including Dorothy de Selincourt, whom he married in 1913, appear as unintentional and unrecognizable caricatures in some of the roles.

In addition to such sketches, Milne perpetrates a series called "Little Plays for Amateurs," whose one distinction is the appropriateness of the title. He attempts to satirize melodrama and sentimental love stories, but he is alternately heavy-handed, arch, coy, snickering, and triter than the objects of his attempted satire. A typical stage direction reads: "Dorothy and Roger embrace each other, if they can do it without causing a scandal in the neighborhood, and the curtain goes down." And another: "The scene is a drawing-room (in which the men are allowed to smoke —or a smoking-room, in which the women are allowed to draw— it doesn't much matter) in the house of somebody or other in the country."

Redeeming moments are rare in such trifles. "The Ordeal By Fire" is a modestly diverting account of Milne's difficulties and final triumph with growing a flame-flower. "The Lucky Month" is a wry little piece about a man whose horoscope tells him that he is "generous to a fault." When he learns that he has accumulated fifty pounds in the bank, he asks his solicitor how he should invest it, and the man says: "I wish you'd lend it to me for a bit." He makes the loan in order to justify his horoscope. "A Matter-of-Fact Fairy Tale," written in the prankish manner later perfected by James Thurber, tickles the fancy and introduces a certain Prince Udo who is turned into a tortoise and whose namesake will reappear in *Once On A Time*, only to be changed into a lion-rabbit-sheep. "Armageddon," reflecting the influence of the war on the hitherto feckless author, achieves literate satire instead of mindless farce; and the poem "Gold Braid" successfully reproduces the idiom of a British Tommy, a little in the style of Siegfried Sassoon, though without his rugged power.

All in all, however, *Those Were the Days* is a faltering apprenticeship and not an attainment. The superficial humor is neither savagely curative like that of Swift nor rooted in universal human foibles like that of Fielding, and it is too contrived and precious even to succeed as farce. The best British humorists of modern times—men like Evelyn Waugh and George Orwell—encompass a judicious blend of topicality, whimsicality, and subtlety. Americans call their humor "dry" because it leans to under- rather than over- statement. The young Milne was reasonably topical (though his topics were slight), tenaciously whimsical, but no more subtle than a bear riding a velocipede.

Nevertheless, Milne enjoyed a considerable vogue in the pages of *Punch* and from the four books collected in *Those Were the Days;* and he helped to popularize a daft, impertinent dialogue which passed for the voice of the young generation newly emancipated from the shackles of Victoria. To some of Milne's compatriots, it was both novel and delightful to hear young people talk slangily and impudently and without regard for the traditions and conventions of their elders. In addition, Milne began his career in the leisurely years before World War I, when wellborn men and women dedicated much of their energy to recreation; and, when they chose to lay down a croquet mallet and pick up a book, they preferred the irrelevancies of a *Punch* essayist to the nobilities of Lord Tennyson.

But the slang and impudence of the young Milne, directed against a queen and an era which have now been so thoroughly exorcised that it is no longer necessary to reject them—indeed, it is possible to view them with nostalgia instead of rancor—have lost their audacity. And his once audacious characters—the Rabbits, Margery and her uncle—seem not so much people as puppets divested of strings and laid in a box for attic storage. *Punch,* which has moved with the times, is as modern as discothéques or as brash as the Beatles. But the early Milne could not have made its pages, much less become an editor.

II   Not That It Matters *and* If I May

Not That It Matters (1919) and *If I May* (1920) are collections of light essays which appeared in the American version of *Vanity Fair* and in the British periodicals *Sphere, Outlook, Daily News,* and *Sunday Express.* Contemporary with the *Punch* pieces collected in *Those Were the Days*—some, in fact, were written as early as 1910—they suffer from the same limitations. With an eye to just such essays, *Twentieth-Century Authors* has remarked of Milne: "But the curse of whimsicality, often of a rather milk-and-water variety, clings to him. . . ."[8]

In itself, of course, the freakish and capricious humor known as whimsy is neither an asset nor a liability. It is possible to be whimsical in many ways: to delight and titillate; to annoy and even nauseate. In the case of the dramatist James Barrie, *Peter Pan* is a triumph of whimsy; *Mary Rose,* a disaster. In the case of Milne, the whimsy of his children's books flows as freely as wine from the fabulous pitcher of Baucis and Philemon. It pervades his scene—the forest of Pooh, the castle of Princess Hyacinth, the hall of Mr. Toad—and envelops his characters in a pink mist of enchantment which piques instead of cloys. But, in his early essays, whimsy is not a mist but a cloud, as thick and finally as nauseating as a surfeit of cotton candy.

Milne once remarked of his early essays that, after he had found a beginning sentence, the other sentences seemed to write themselves. Indeed, they have such a look. They accumulate whimsicalities without point or relevance. Familiar essayists such as Charles Lamb and Robert Louis Stevenson often ramble down whimsical bypaths. The reader who follows their lead is more than content to forego a direct route, secure in the knowledge that his guides are leading him, circuitously but charmingly, to a worthwhile destination. The freedom of the genre, the fact that it may be discursive and personal, is one of its charms. Milne, unfortunately, rambles until he gets lost. In "Midsummer Day," which begins with the observation that magic inhabits the woods in the summer, the reader who expects an essay about such magic is soon disillusioned. He receives a lengthy digression, bristling with puns, on the migratory habits of the cuckoo: "Where he goes I know not, but I think of him vaguely as at Mozambique, a paradise for all good birds who like their days long. If geography were properly taught at schools, I should know where Mozambique was, and what sort of people live there. But it may be that, with all these cuckoos cuckooing and swallows swallowing from

July to April, the country is so full of immigrants that there is no
room for a stable population. It may also be, of course, that
Mozambique is not the place I am thinking of; yet it has a bird-
ish sound."[9] Eventually, and by means of a route which includes
an altogether gratuitous visit with caterpillars, and which is so
tortuous that it might better be called a maze, he returns to midsummer day. Like a dragonfly, he has flickered from subject to
subject, and his subjects have been the paper flowers of whimsy,
brightly painted but without scent or substance.

Indirection is not Milne's only failing. He cultivates a foppish
and even snobbish image of himself as a clotheshorse and bon
vivant. He may pretend to be joking when he remarks that
"choosing a flannel suit in May is one of the moments of one's
life," but he makes such remarks so often that he appears to mean
exactly what he says: "For one thing I have my best clothes on,"
"All London is now gazing at my old top-hat," or "Have you
ordered your half-hose yet?" A familiar essayist succeeds insofar
as he engages the reader with his personality, since, as Milne was
quick to admit, the essays are the man. Milne, the clotheshorse, is
no more animated than a mannequin in a department store; and
the essays which frame and enclose him, as a window encloses the
mannequin, are at once garishly illuminated and glassily cold.

To be sure, a few of his essays move directly to valid points. In
"By the Sea," he dramatizes the inclination of the old to suppose
that not themselves but world is aging, failing, fading. He concludes with ironic insistence, "I shall maintain that it is the sea
which is not what it was." But Lamb, Milne's favorite model as
an essayist, who has treated the same subject much more skillfully
in "Old China," stabs the heart with wistfulness as well as the
brain with irony. All of the wry wisdom of age, and also the
knowledge that wisdom is no substitute for youth, resounds in
Lamb's sigh to Mary: "It is true we were happier when we were
poorer, but we were also younger, my cousin." The difference between the two essays is that between adequacy and greatness.

In spite of numerous failures and occasional adequacies, however, the two collections include Milne's first literary criticism and
a strong presentiment of the critic to come. In *Not That It Matters*, he draws a portrait of "The Ideal Author" as the public sees
him and sadly notes that "a layman will never take an author
quite seriously. He regards authorship, not as a profession, but as

something between an inspiration and a hobby. In as far as it is an inspiration, it is a gift from Heaven, and ought to be shared with the rest of the world; in as far as it is a hobby, it is something which should be done not too expertly, but in a casual, amateur, haphazard fashion."[10] In *If I May*, he includes an essay called "The Robinson Tradition" which suggests that the weakness of the *Swiss Family Robinson* is the presence of the parents; and the weakness of Captain Marryat's *Masterman Ready* is not only the presence of parents but of one who moralizes. No boy, however dutiful and affectionate, wants his mother and father to share his desert island since the purpose of the island is to isolate him from rules and responsibilities. The few pieces of literary criticism in *If I May* and *Not That It Matters* indicate that Milne has served his apprenticeship and developed a clean, spare style and a perspicacious eye. When the right subject presents itself, he can meet its demands. Happily, his next collection, *By Way of Introduction*, sparkles with right subjects, most of them literary.

III   By Way of Introduction

By Way of Introduction was published in 1929, when Milne had achieved fame not only as a dramatist but as the creator of Christopher Robin and Pooh. He was celebrated enough to be invited by his publisher, Methuen, to introduce books by other authors, and he was popular enough for the introductions he wrote for his own books to enhance their value for readers who liked to feel themselves admitted to the secret processes of composition. In addition to introductions, the volume contains reviews of books by such writers as George Jean Nathan, Brander Matthews, Karel Capek, Saki, and A. Conan Doyle, and also a group of essays on such varied subjects as spiritualism, children's stories, exchanging presents, and the genesis of the Christopher Robin poems.

By Way of Introduction introduces Milne, the man, in the new flattering light of maturity. Gone is the empty-brained, foppish young editor of *Punch* who seemed to spend more time at house parties than at the office. He still writes occasionally about parties, cricket, and golf, but the subject of recreation is less important than that of creation: how books are created and why they are written; why they succeed or fail. He defines the dramatist as "both artist and craftsman. He is a stage-craftsman by reason of the fact that he collaborates with the public. To put it vulgarly, every play is a bluff. Things didn't happen so, and couldn't happen so; but the dramatist is going to bluff the audience into believing (for three hours anyway) that things did happen so."[11] He applauds the illustrations of Ernest H. Shepard, who illustrated Kenneth Grahame's Wind in the Willows and whose Christopher Robin, long of hair, round of hat, bumptious of disposition, became inseparable from Milne's poems: "every mother prays simply for a little Shepard child, and leaves it to Mr. Shepard whether it is a boy or a girl. . . ."[12] Milne even finds time to defend fairy tales against the assaults of scientific materialism: "To say that a child has no need for fairies when there are so many beautiful birds and butterflies in the world, or no need for seven-league boots so long as five and five most wonderfully make ten, is like saying that a man has no need for Switzerland until he has exhausted (as none of us have) the beauties of England, nor any need for Wordsworth until he has mastered every line of Shakespeare."[13]

Always readable on the work of others, whether about plays, pictures, or fairy tales, Milne is even more readable about himself —the subject he knows best. His tributes to other writers are interspersed with allusions to his own tastes and methods. For instance, in his introduction to Saki's Chronicles of Clovis, he admits that he once tried to imitate that "strange, exotic creature" but had to content himself with "collar-studs and hot-water bottles" instead of "were-wolves and tigers," and with wondering ignobly "if it were not much easier to be funny with tigers than with collar-studs; if Saki's careless cruelty, that strange boyish insensitiveness of his, did not give an unfair start in the pursuit of laughter."[14]

He is most revealing, of course, in the introductions which he wrote to his own books. It is dangerous for a writer to introduce himself in print: he risks the Scylla of egotism if he claims merits which are not apparent, and The Charybdis of false modesty if he disclaims merits which are readily apparent. In some of his uncollected introductions—particularly those to his plays—he succumbs to either the ravening jaws or the clashing rocks. But here he avoids both risks with a mixture of candor and canniness worthy of Ulysses. He frankly confesses that he felt "amazement and disgust" when he, the author of the Christopher Robin books, was totally eclipsed by his youthful hero. It seems that his own childhood, as well as that of his son, had inspired the books; but the public discovered Christopher in every poem and clutched him to their hearts like his teddy bear, Pooh. But then, before Milne can be accused of begrudging the limelight to his son, he gives him credit for having created Pooh and friends: "He and his mother gave them life, and I have just 'put them into a book."[15]

By Way of Introduction introduces a frank and articulate author who has read and written some excellent books, and who has written about them with the excellence which they deserve. He always felt that his essays were incidental to his plays, but the public considered them as incidental to his juveniles. But *By Way of Introduction*, still in print, has proved more durable than most of the plays, and it frames and vivifies the juveniles which it cannot equal.

IV   The Ascent of Man, Peace with Honour, War with
Honour, *and* War Aims Unlimited

Peace with Honour, subtitled *An Inquiry into the War Convention*, consists of eighteen connected but largely independent chapters written from 1933 to 1935, when militant forces in England and France seemed almost as war-minded as the dictators of Italy and Germany. Milne himself, having fought in World War I, had seen the havoc of its battles and the emptiness of its peace. Then, in 1928, in the pamphlet *The Ascent of Man*, he had described God as the indefinable and unknowable power whom man could best worship by making the most of earth instead of contemplating heaven. To worship such a God, he had argued, it was necessary to eliminate war. In *Peace with Honour*, he elaborates his viewpoint and proclaims himself a dedicated pacifist.

To many men, Milne charges, national prestige is no more than a will to war and a nation's honor is measured by its willingness to use force. On the contrary, prestige should be a will to *peace;* honor should be measured by a willingness to *renounce* force. In the time of Napoleon, war was largely confined to fleets and armies, to sailors and soldiers who were trained to fight and prepared to die. There were no airplanes to bomb civilians; no submarines to torpedo passenger liners; the bright uniforms and

burnished muskets, the code of the gentleman warrior, were not
without their glory. But modern war is worse than inglorious: it
is legalized bestiality.

Having stated his case against war, Milne proposes a plan for
peace. He imagines himself addressing the assembled leaders of
England, France, Italy, and Germany, and he exhorts both the
leaders and their people to take an irrevocable oath "to renounce
aggressive *and defensive* war, and to submit *all* disputes to arbi-
tration." He concedes that the leaders are neither particularly
intelligent, humane, nor honorable, but "that they are just intelligent enough to realize that another European war will mean complete disaster for the world; just humane enough to wish to save
Europe from the untellable horror of this war; just honourable
enough, when they have taken a solemn oath to save Europe, to
intend to keep their word."[16] But, if Germany should violate the
oath, build armaments, and occupy a trusting and defenseless
England, Milne's answer is unequivocal: "England would have
lost something . . . but she would not have lost her honour." In
other words, better conquered than dishonored. Thus, with a
slight variation, he anticipates the Ban the Bombers of the 1950's,
whose slogan was "Better Red than Dead."

Regrettably, the Great Men of Europe—at least some of them—
proved even less intelligent, humane, and honorable than Milne
had anticipated. Hitler, Mussolini, and Stalin violated many
agreements; and there is no reason to think that, having pledged
themselves to renounce war, they would have honored their
pledge any more than Germany respected the boundaries of
Poland, or Russia the borders of Finland. It may also be questioned if an occupied England could have found much comfort
in honor when the conquerors were Nazi Storm Troopers. Though
Milne recognized the brutalities of modern war, he failed to
recognize that occupation could be as brutal as conquest. In spite
of its eloquently phrased and admirably organized arguments, its
idealism and its unquestionable sincerity, *Peace with Honour* did
not convince Milne's own countrymen. Viewed today in the after-
math of World War II and the shadow of a possible World War
III, his ideal for peace is still commendable but his means to
achieve peace seems, at best, naïve; at worst, meaningless. Sacred
oaths are momentary conveniences to nations which cultivate
deceit as a guiding principle and which regard Machiavelli as a

mere preface to Marx and Lenin. At one time, Milne considered *Peace with Honour* his finest book, but the realities of World War II and the actual threat of Nazi invasion showed him the inadequacy of his arguments.

War with Honour, a thirty-two page pamphlet published in 1940, and *War Aims Unlimited*, a forty-one page pamphlet published in 1941, are his answers to *Peace with Honour*. Faced with the barbarisms of Hitler, he admits that his plea for pacifism must now be sharply revised. "If anybody reads *Peace with Honour* now, he must read it with that one word 'HITLER' scrawled across every page. Before every irresistible conclusion to which I seek to draw him he must insert another premise: 'HITLER.' "[17] Nazi rule, he has come to believe, "is the foulest abomination with which mankind has ever been faced," and he also warns against the Communists who promise a New Order after the defeat of Hitler but whose order is only new in substituting communism for fascism. Milne remains, he insists, in theory a pacifist; but the time to work for peace is between wars and not in the midst of a war whose horrors stagger the imagination. "I said in a previous chapter that the war demanded greater sacrifice from us than we realized. It has demanded from me, not only my butter and bacon, but my pacifism."[18]

Judged as essays, *War with Honour* and *War Aims Unlimited* are vastly inferior to *Peace with Honour*. Written with haste and with more fervor than style, they could better have been condensed and organized into a single pamphlet. Furthermore, they apply specifically and narrowly to the first years of World War II; in the 1960's, it is no longer instructive to be informed, as if with sudden discovery, that Hitler is a devil who has perverted the youth of Germany. Except for the still timely warning of the essays against the deviousness of communism, they are little more than sincere but dated journalism. They deserve respect as courageous confessions of a change in conviction—as confessions, but not as literature.

V Year In, Year Out

Year In, Year Out, Milne's last book, is a random collection published in 1952, when the author was seventy. A few of the pieces had gone uncollected for thirty years; most of them were fairly recent and were ripe with the mellowness of a man to whom autumn meant fulfillment and not decay. In the author's words, the book is a "calendar of disconnected ideas," and its arrangement under the twelve months is often arbitrary, an essay on conversation appearing under July for no good reason except that the month is part of the social season in London. The arbitrariness, however, is not the purposeless indirection of his early essays, the erratic skimmings of a dragonfly among paper flowers. A dragonfly he remains, but his flowers are vivid and fragrant; and he leaves behind him a dust of fertilizing pollen of good sense and keen sensibilities. *Year In, Year Out* is a gracious and graceful farewell to the audience which had followed him faithfully through his long career, had sometimes maddened him by forgetting that he had created Mr. Pim as well as Pooh, but had never denied him a chance to speak.

There is a brief, brilliant appreciation of Lewis Carroll and the wish that he had not diminished his wonderland by treating Alice's adventures as a dream: "For who is ever interested in somebody else's dream?"[19] There is the serious suggestion that the Old Testament should be excluded from the Christian Bible— admired as literature but condemned for its religious, or rather irreligious, teachings, most of which run exactly counter to the gentler precepts of the New Testament. There are comments on the difference between a good dramatist and a good novelist: "It is the business of the dramatist to be aware of the audience, as it is not the business of the novelist to be aware of the reader. The reason why many novelists who are great artists (Stevenson and James, for instance) have not been great dramatists is that they have not been aware of their audience; that is, they have written their plays as artists only, not as craftsmen."[20] There is a further clarification of his pacifism: he is still a pacifist in that he ardently desires peace; but, having called for wholehearted resistance to Hitler in 1940, he now endorses the atom bomb as a deterrent to communism. "The atom bomb is a weapon, not for victory in war, not for 'pairing' with the enemy in war, but to prevent war. To be prepared so to use it demands courage: the courage Samson showed when he pulled down the pillars of the temple."[21]

The playful Milne is also at hand—the genuine humorist, not the farceur—his fun undiminished by the passage of years. Wryly he tells of his first meeting with George Bernard Shaw, who much earlier had seen Milne's play *Belinda* and who now said, "eagerly, as if he had been brooding about it for five years and was glad to get it off his mind: 'You know, your Belinda was a minx, that's what she was, she was a minx!'"[22] Milne imagines under what circumstances Bacon might have written the poems and plays attributed to Shakespeare and then prevailed on a country lout from Stratford to sign his name to them. He dashes off an observation about birds in a style associated with Ogden Nash but perfected by Milne as early as the Christopher Robin poems:

A great many words
Have been written about birds;
From rhapsody (Shelley's)
To more precise information about the colour of their bellies.[23]

In short, *Year In, Year Out* is the self-portrait of a writer successful but not boastful—wise but not sententious, aging but not old—who for half a century, from his first adolescent trillings in *Punch* to this, his farewell without tears, has spoken his mind through the medium of his essays.

CHAPTER 2

Drawing Rooms and Dreams

"THE MOST EXCITING form of writing," wrote Milne, "is the writing of plays." A novel "continuously demands from the author paragraphs, sometimes whole pages, in whose composition no delight can be taken"; but a play, except for the "dreary work" of inserting the stage directions, offers to the dramatist the challenge and the reward of creating action and dialogue which, in the mirror of the stage, distort real life so as best to reflect its meaning.[1]

Milne began his career as a dramatist at the age of nine when, together with his brother Ken and a friend Charles, he read and dramatized a threepenny novel called *The Golden Key*. Naturally aureoled with golden curls, Milne cast himself in the role of the young governess beloved by bold Lord Marchmont. Though his acting fell short of his looks, he remained for the rest of his life a devotee of the stage. It was many years, however, before he could begin his theatrical career in earnest. Established as an essayist and editor, self-supporting and reasonably popular, he hesitated to invade a new and difficult field. To write plays was to jeopardize his security and to risk oblivion: written, the plays might be ignored by producers; produced, they might not succeed on the stage. Only in the army during World War I, while stationed on the Isle of Wight as a signalling officer, did he find the time and the daring to write his first full-length play. He was asked by his colonel to compose a skit in which the colonel's children might entertain the personnel of the base. He never fulfilled the assignment for the children, but in 1916, with the help of his wife Daphne, to whom he dictated dialogue, he did compose an adult farce called *Wurzel-Flummery*, which opened for an eight-week run on the London stage in 1917 and which brought him a royalty of thirty pounds a week.

After the war, Milne announced to Daphne that he did not

intend to resume his duties with *Punch*. For one thing, someone
had taken his job as assistant editor; for another, he hoped to
become a full-time dramatist. Daphne burst into tears. Perhaps
she felt that a career launched by such an unballasted and unsea-
worthy vessel as *Wurzel-Flummery* was doomed to capsize with
the first gust of wind. She was mistaken. After the brilliant success of *Mr. Pim Passes By* in 1920, fashionable London was quot-
ing Milne's epigrams and great actresses like Ethel Barrymore
and Irene Vanbrugh were vying to play his glamorous, garrulous
heroines. Anthologists began to include his work in definitive collections, and critics began to discuss him in the same paragraph,
if not the same breath, with Barrie and Shaw.

But Milne's quality did not keep pace with his popularity. As
early as 1923 the American critic George Jean Nathan diagnosed
his crippling limitations and chose him as the best exemplar of
the "lesser British playwrights," who, he felt, suffered "from their
heavy effort to be insistently light. Their lightness has about it
not infrequently a sense of tug and strain. . . . The net impression
that one takes away from their exhibits, consequently, is a sense
of having been present at a dinner party whereat all the exceptionally dull guests have endeavored to be assiduously amusing."[2]
(Ironically, Milne was asked to review Nathan's book and wrote
a mild report.) Time has proved the justice of Nathan's estimate.
After Milne's *Second Plays* in 1921, he ceased to develop as a
dramatist and, for the most part, contented himself with lavishing
careful craftsmanship on borrowed materials.

He wrote in the long tradition of the drawing-room comedy,
which had flourished and scintillated with William Congreve,
Joseph Sheridan, and Oscar Wilde but started to falter with Barrie and Maugham; and, much less frequently, Milne wrote in the
newer tradition of the "problem play," as practiced by Henrik
Ibsen, Arthur Pinero, John Galsworthy, and G. B. Shaw, who
faced their heroes and heroines with conflicts arising from the
urgencies of modern society, its politics, its mores, its neuroses.
Most of Milne's characters, however, whether treated comically
or seriously, belong in the drawing rooms of British society; they
are or aspire to be aristocrats.

Milne's own forebears were neither rich nor titled. His great-
grandfather was a stone mason; his grandfather was a Presby-
terian minister notable for his charity to everyone except the

members of his own family; and his self-educated father was a clerk in a counting house, an apprentice in an engineering firm, a schoolmaster, and finally the owner of Henley House, an unpretentious and unprofitable school for some fifty boys from eight to eighteen. But Milne's father managed to prepare his son for a higher social stratum: with the help of scholarships, he sent him first to Westminster and then to Cambridge. Milne—as a young man about town who had gone to the right schools and who, at the age of twenty-four, had joined the staff of *Punch*—was tirelessly cultivated by London hostesses with marriageable daughters and whisked to the great country houses whose fiefdoms included golf links, private lakes, and game preserves.

Perhaps because he was adopted into rather than born to the manner, he responded with a curious mingling of awe and irony. The people he saw seemed polished, confident, and glamorous; and he envied and sometimes imitated them. At the same time, he recognized their limitations, their smugness, and their subservience to outworn traditions. Whether awed or ironic, however, he never tired of writing about them. He wrote most of his plays between the two world wars, before the country houses had become museums for American tourists, and their owners, burdened with taxes, had been reduced to the role of caretakers and lodged in the gamekeeper's or the gardener's cottage. Probably his audiences realized that the old, unhurried life of the town house and the country house was threatened by the fiercely equalizing pressures of modern society—women's suffrage, the rise of labor, the blurring of class distinctions—and doomed to the fate of mammoths, dodoes, and carrier pigeons. But they clung to the past with nostalgic tenacity, and Milne, more tenacious than most of his audience, fed their nostalgia with plays which allowed his set and costume designers to dazzle the eye, and his full-throated actors and actresses to bemuse the ear, even when his plots and some of his lines were as dated as the Crystal Palace.

Like Oscar Wilde, Milne satirized society and loved what he satirized. But, unlike Wilde, Milne as a dramatist has gathered dust along with his drawing rooms. Amid his dark, ornate, and overabundant furniture, his plethora of portraits and landscapes, chaise longues, and presentation clocks, move people whose manners seem as elaborate and artificial as a rococo chair. Sharp-tongued dowagers deliver advice with the self-importance of

Cumaean Sibyls, and bland, faultlessly dressed gentlemen expand their meagre energies in the pursuit of idleness. Servants, gliding through the ancient ritual of "Yes, my Lord" and "No, my Lady," maintain a sphinxlike imperturbability even when faced with the fact that Lady X is living in sin or Lord Y intends a seduction.

Such a way of life is incalculably remote in mood, if not in years, from the Beatlemania, the Ban on Bombers, the Mods and the Rockers of modern England. After all, John Osborne has looked back in anger; Alan·Sillitoe has shown a young roughneck on Saturday night and Sunday morning; and Shelagh Delaney has served a taste of honey which to the palates of Milne's contemporaries would have seemed a taste of bitters. To Americans, with no widespread tradition of country houses and class distinctions, such a life is more than remote; it is unimaginable.

Wilde, on the other hand, has survived by dint of his wits, or rather, his wit. His plots creak, his country houses glisten with cobwebs, but Lady Bracknell has not lost her venom, and the loss of Lady Windemere's fan is still the occasion for epigrams which sparkle and thrust like the damascene blades of Damascus. Wilde has weathered disgrace and censorship to delight the grandchildren of the generation which sent him to prison and banned his plays. Not for nothing did Milne confess that the play he would most have liked to write was *The Importance of Being Earnest.* But Milne has no play to approach the best of his master; Milne, of whom Nathan wrote: "An irrelative allusion to pigs interjected suddenly into a conversation on love, an alien reference to sausages inserted into an observation on cynicism, an extraneous mention of a bowler hat during a discussion of poetry—these are the species of comic gold-fish that such playwrights as A. A. Milne, for example, continually pull out of their silk hats."[3] "Comic goldfish" are insufficient to keep a modern audience from noticing the flimsiness of Milne's hats. The silk has frayed and faded. It was, on the whole, synthetic from the start, and not the work of knowledgeable silkworms.

Happily, a handful of plays deserve to be expected from Nathan's condemnation: *Mr. Pim Passes By,* whose drawing room opens its doors to the fresh airs of modernity in the person of Olivia, Milne's most enchanting heroine; the uneven but sometimes brilliant literary puzzle, *The Truth About Blayds;* the fairytale plays, *Portrait of a Gentleman in Slippers, The Ugly Duck-*

ling, *The Ivory Door,* and *Toad of Toad Hall,* which deliver us from dull English aristocrats and into the hands of their comelier prototypes, the kings and princesses of make-believe. But, all in all, when the good and enduring are weighed against the bad, dull, and derivative, the plays of Milne are a barren Sinai in which the manna of excellence is delectable but much too infrequent for a sustaining diet.

I First Plays

The first of Milne's *First Plays* (1919), *Wurzel-Flummery,* succeeded in reaching the stage through the intervention of James Barrie, the living dramatist whom he most admired and to whom he repeatedly acknowledged a "great debt." In 1910, Milne had mailed to Barrie a copy of his *Punch* essays collected as *The Day's Play.* Barrie, impressed, had invited the young essayist to lunch and ended by becoming his friend and patron. Seven years later he liked *Wurzel-Flummery* enough to arrange for a production under the auspices of Dion George Boucicault.

Wurzel-Flummery was written with three acts, reduced to two for Boucicault's production, and trimmed to one for publication in *First Plays.* Since the plot is hardly sufficient to inspire an anecdote, even the one-act version seems interminable as Milne asks and answers the less than electrifying question: "Will a man of honor assume a name like Wurzel-Flummery in order to receive an inheritance of fifty thousand pounds?" An eccentric by the name of Antony Clifton, who likes to expose the venery of politicians, draws a will in which he offers that sum to each of two violently opposed Members of Parliament. Since both men are vain of their hard-won reputations, both pretend to be shocked and outraged by the implication that they might change their names in order to receive an inheritance. At the end of the play, however, there are two Wurzel-Flummerys.

For once, a plot summary can do justice to a play; for nothing is lost by reducing the entire act to a single paragraph. Wurzel-Flummery recalls those flavorless dialogues, "Little Plays for Amateurs," which Milne contributed to *Punch,* except that it is longer and even more labored. The one notable line is spoken by the eccentric's nephew, Denis Clifton, who aspires to authorship and resents the accusation that he writes farces. "Not farces, comedies—of a whimsical nature," he protests; and the same might be said of Milne's fairy-tale plays. But not of *Wurzel-Flummery*, which, lacking high spirits, lightness, suppleness, and spontaneity, is not a comedy, not even a good farce, but an unmitigated bore. Milne's second play, the three-act *Lucky One*, surpasses *Wurzel-Flummery* in merit as well as in length. Ironically, it was never produced in London, perhaps because, in the author's words, "the girl marries the wrong man." Gerald Farringdon is a handsome and popular young gentleman-about-town, and at first he seems to be the "lucky one" of the title, while his older brother Bob, plain, stolid, slow to make friends, appears to be his unlucky opposite. When the play opens, we learn that Bob has just lost his girl Pamela to Gerald and, what is more, that he is threatened with prison because his business partner has absconded with the company funds. But, when Bob goes to jail, Bob wins Pamela's sympathy, recovers her love, and marries her after his release. Thus, the "lucky one" loses both his girl and his luck to his luckless brother.

A good play asks a question, poses a problem, raises a doubt; and the doubt in *The Lucky One* is whether the handsome Gerald or the suffering Bob deserves the luck. We are shown an underdog, victimized, it seems, by fickle love and false friendship, and our sympathies rush to support him in his misfortunes. Then we pause and ask ourselves the question: are we not sentimentalizing him simply because he is unattractive and unloved, and rejecting his brother, Gerald, simply because he is charming, capable, and beloved? At the end, we realize that Gerald is truly the worthier brother, that his charm, far from superficial, reflects his character, and that Bob is petty, mean, and selfish, the victim not of misfortune but of misused fortune. Apropos of *The Lucky One*, Milne wrote in his autobiography: "I used to think it was my best play. Well, I suppose it was once; but now I see that I just wasted a good idea."[4] Perhaps he meant that he had failed to make the sympathetic Pamela anything more than a device to test the brothers, and had also failed to hint at Gerald's true character until it was nearly too late to save him in the esteem of the audience. Nonetheless, as a play which punctures illusion with the pinpricks of irony, *The Lucky One* is almost successful and altogether promising.

Milne's next play, however, the one-act *Boy Comes Home*, for-

sakes irony for the somber fantasy known as Expressionism.
Milne, who excelled as a fantasist only when he was playful, had
no gift for the dark dreamscapes which haunt the paintings of
such Expressionist painters as Munch and Ensor and such plays
of August Strindberg as *The Ghost Sonata*. Milne, ill at ease with
nightmares of the soul, circles them warily and recoils from their
implications. Philip, the boy of the title, comes home from war to
his domineering uncle and guardian, James. But the boy, once
meek and biddable, has changed in the trenches. When James
asks him to enter his business, Philip refuses; he wants to be an
architect and requests the money left to him by his father. James
replies coldly: "You come into your money when you are twenty-
five." If it comes to that, answers Philip, he *is* "twenty-five . . . or
forty-five." Gradually, the room assumes the unreality of a battlefield, and Philip begins to talk like a lunatic. Babbling of war and
carnage, he draws a revolver and threatens to fire—then he produces a hand grenade and threatens to pull the pin. The terrified
James agrees to give him his money. At this point, James "opens
his eyes with a start" and, finding himself alone in his own drawing room, tries to dismiss the episode as a dream. In walks Philip
with a piece of toast and docilely agrees to enter his uncle's business. But, asks Milne in the final stage directions, "Was it a dream,
or wasn't it?"

If it was not a dream, then Philip's agreement to enter the family business is inconsistent with his wish to be an architect. The
war, it would seem, has taught him nothing. If it was a dream,
then Milne has committed the blunder for which he criticized
Lewis Carroll in *Alice in Wonderland* telling a tale and then,
as if by way of apology, tucking its wonders into the mind of a
dreamer. First played at the Victoria Palace in London, *The Boy
Comes Home* was later performed in numerous little theaters;
but timeliness and not excellence must be held accountable for
its great, if short-lived, popularity. It is the one play which Milne
wrote about World War I; he hated the war and wars in general
far too much to find them congenial materials for his pen.

His next play, *Belinda*, reverts to the farce of *Wurzel-Flummery*. Duller by two additional acts, hurriedly written in six eve-
nings, it survived for nine weeks on the London stage only
through the grace and skill of its leading lady, the celebrated
Irene Vanbrugh, wife of the same Boucicault who had produced

Wurzel-Flummery. Belinda, a beautiful woman in the late summer of life, employs the wiles of spring to attract a middle-aged statistician and a long-haired young poet. But Belinda has two secrets: a nubile daughter, Delia, and a lost husband, Tremayne. Her daughter returns from studies in Paris; her husband, from assorted wanderings. After several moronic dialogues in which Belinda is kittenish and Tremayne is dogged, the two are reconciled and reunited; Delia marries the poet; and the statistician returns to his statistics.

Milne remarked of Belinda: "She was the heroine of a purely artificial comedy whose only purpose was to amuse, and she herself no closer to reality than any character in, say, *The Importance of Being Earnest*."[5] Belinda does not achieve her modest purpose. If Milne had provided her with Wildean wit, she might have justified her artificiality; like Lady Windemere, unbelievable but irresistible, she might have sparkled and possibly bewitched. Perhaps Irene Vanbrugh in London and Ethel Barrymore in America gave to her lines a tease and blitheness missing from the mere printed words. But a published play should tease in its own right; when subtitled *An April Folly*, it promises to exhale the scent of dogwood and to ring with the merry accents of the cuckoo. As it is, *Belinda* is little April but much folly.

The fifth and last of Milne's *First Plays* is *The Red Feathers*, a one-act operetta without music. A mother and daughter inhabit a rustic country house, half farm, half manor, in "any year you please—between, let us say, the day when the fiddle first came to England and the day when Romance left it." The mother, surfeited with life, is content to drift with the seasons in her pleasant house. But her daughter sits at a spinet and sings a wistful song. Her constant lament is, "Perhaps one day something will happen." Something happens in the guise of three traveling players, the Red Feathers—a plump philosopher called the Talker; a younger, slimmer man, the Singer; and a quiet, pretty girl, the Fiddler— who come to beg dinner with songs of the open road and end by staying for many dinners and many days. At length, the Singer proposes to the girl, the Talker to her mother, and both men decide to forsake the road and live in the cottage with their wives. Only the Fiddler, who has no sweetheart, returns to her wanderings.

An operetta without music is like that flightless bird, the emu;

unable to fly, it must struggle along the ground. But the ground
in *Three Feathers* is scenic if not exciting. The lyrics are grace-
fully tinkling even without accompaniment, and the speeches are
mannered and decorative in the fashion of a Theocritan dialogue.
More important, the air of make-believe which envelops the cottage, the once-upon-a-time of "any year you please," foretells the
fairy-tale plays to come, *The Ivory Door* and *Toad of Toad Hall*.
First Plays—burdened though the collection is with the foolishness
of *Wurzel-Flummery* and *Belinda* and with the uncertainties of
The Boy Comes Home—almost make amends with *The Lucky
One* and *The Red Feathers* and promises additional plays which
are more than a promise.

II   Second Plays

Second Plays, written between 1918 and 1920 and collected in
1921, are not only incomparably better than *First* but also much
the best of Milne's four collections. Critics and public, remember-
ing *Wurzel-Flummery*, praised Milne's growth as a dramatist and,
unable to foresee that he would cease to grow, hailed him as the
bright Aldebaran of the theatrical firmament, if not quite a Sirius-
like George Bernard Shaw. What is more, *Mr. Pim Passes By* not
only delighted its audience but brought to its author a considerable fortune and amply justified him in his decision to renounce
the security of *Punch*.

Make-Believe, which opens the volume, was the first play
which he wrote especially for children—in a sense, it is the long-
delayed fruit of the colonel's assignment on the Isle of Wight—
and a youthful Herbert Marshall played several roles in the first
production at the Lyric Theatre, Hammersmith. In his Prologue,
Milne imagines the nine Hubbard children, their friend Rose-
mary, and the butler James as gathered in the drawing room to
think the kind of adventures which they would like to see on the
stage. The three acts which follow the Prologue represent their
thoughts translated into three separate stories. "The Princess and
the Woodcutter" tells of a woodcutter who vies with three princes
for the hand of a beautiful princess. To test the hearts of the
suitors, the girl's mother, the queen, disguises herself as an old
beggar woman and begs each of the princes for a crust of bread.
The woodcutter manages to supply each prince with a very dry

crust. After she has dutifully eaten the crusts, the queen is wracked with thirst, and the woodcutter opportunely appears with a flagon of wine and wins both her gratitude and the hand of her daughter.

The second act, "Oliver's Island," recounts the adventures of a small boy named Oliver and his sister Jill who escape from dull relatives and a sermonizing minister to rule a pirate's island, where relatives are reduced to servants and where the minister, now a missionary, is pursued, divided, and devoured by a cannibal and a cassowary. The third act, "Father Christmas and the Hubbard Family," recalls the visit of Mr. and Mrs. Hubbard to the mansion of Father Christmas and the present they received in return for their courtesy: the nine little Hubbards who are now their children.

Make-Believe is no *Peter Pan*. As the title suggests, it wears an apologetic air of being made up, of existing only in the children's minds and not on the stage. Too often the reader feels as if he is still in the Hubbards' drawing room instead of in the enchanted forest with the woodcutter, on the island of the pirates, or visiting Father Christmas. "The difficulty in the way of writing a children's play," wrote Milne, "is that Barrie was born too soon."[6] Nonetheless, *Make-Believe* has moments and scenes of inimitable charm; and its portraits of children, even to the gruesome touch of Oliver's and Jill's wanting to see "who gets most" when the cannibal and the bird pursue the missionary, are unsentimentalized and psychologically sound. Like *The Red Feathers*, it anticipates the later fairy-tale plays in which Milne creates magic—not make-believe.

Mr. Pim Passes By, originally titled *Green Curtains*, is more than a foretaste of excellence: it is a brilliant and somehow timeless drawing-room comedy, a play which deserved its early success and deserves renewed attention. Presented in London with Irene Vanbrugh and Leslie Howard in leading roles, it proved the theatrical event of 1920; and Milne, the leading lady, and her husband, the producer Boucicault (who also appeared as Mr. Pim), were summoned onto the stage for so many curtain calls that a weary stagehand growled to him: " 'Ere, go on and give 'em a speech, guv'nor, and let's all go 'ome."[7] It was always to be the play with which Milne was most frequently associated, and he liked to tell a wry story about his introduction to a world golf

champion: "Our introducer, wishing to do his best for me, added
kindly, 'The writer, you know.' The golfer looked uncomfortable
and said, 'Oh, yes.' I should have been content to leave it there,
but my friend was more persistent. 'You know,' he said doggedly;
'the dramatist, Mr. Pim Passes By.' Amazingly the golfer's face
lit up. He beamed at me. 'Oh,' he said eagerly, 'then you know a
lot of actresses!' "[8]

In 1921 Milne adapted Mr. Pim Passes By into his finest novel,
which preserves the best of the dialogue and illuminates it with
the descriptions and the interior monologues permitted to a novelist but not to a dramatist. Reading the play, we must visualize
the enchanting Olivia through her speeches and through the
gently stubborn persuasion with which she humanizes her stolid
husband. Reading the novel, we may see her as she appears to the
author: idealized, yes, but not marbleized; womanly as well as
heavenly; Milne's wife with another name. In a word, the novel
enlarges rather than attenuates the virtues of the play; and the
characters, plot, and theme are better reserved for consideration in
Chapter 7.

The final long play in the collection, The Romantic Age, though
less than a Mr. Pim Passes By, is a kind of Make-Believe for
adults. The heroine is a young girl named Melisande who, faithful
to her archaistic name, yearns for the lost age of chivalry. People
insist on calling her Sandy; a dull young man, a sportsman and
would-be financier, insists on proposing to her. But Melisande is
waiting for a prince, and her patience is soon rewarded. Early
one morning, when dew is on the leaves and mist is in the air,
she walks into the forest and meets a young man named Gervase
who is dressed in blue and gold like a knight from Camelot. Actually, he is dressed for a costume ball; he has spent the night in the
woods because his car has stalled; but to Melisande he is her long
awaited lover. When she sees him again, however, coming to call
on her father, he is wearing a loud golfing suit and he cheerfully
confesses that he is a member of the Stock Exchange.

No longer a prince, he seems to her indistinguishable from all
the dull, golf-playing young businessmen she meets at subscrip-
tion dances. Coldly she rejects his attempts to regain the rapture
which they shared in the forest. But Gervase wisely replies:
"There's romance everywhere if you look for it. You look for it in
the old fairy-stories, but did they find it there? . . . In two

thousand or two hundred thousand years, people will read stories
about *us,* and sigh and say, 'Will those romantic days never come
back again?' Ah, they are here now, Melisande, for *us;* for the
people with imagination; for you and for me.'"⁹ Who could resist
such a plan? Not Melisande. When Gervase leaves her, sure to
return, of course, and assured of a welcome, she opens a cook
book and begins to read a recipe as if it were an incantation:
"Take an onion, peel and quarter it, and simmer it in milk. . . ."

When critics complained that no one behaved like Melisande
in modern England, Milne replied that there was still a type of
girl "who in her heart, secretly, thinks like this"; that the only
way a dramatist can suggest his heroine's thoughts is to express
them in her behavior and conversation, since, unlike a novelist,
he is not allowed to look into her mind. Doubtless he is right. No
one could call the twentieth century a romantic age—indeed, it is
called the Age of Anxiety—and yet there are Melisandes by other
names who dream of knights but settle for Gervases and learn to
invest their mundane tasks with a sheen of wonder. Milne's play,
addressed to just such girls, is a dreamer's warning that they must
adapt their dreams to realities—adapt but not diminish them.

Milne has aptly written of the two one-act plays—*The Camberly Triangle* and *The Stepmother*—which complete and mar his
otherwise impressive volume, that "nothing much need be said."
The Camberly Triangle consists of a fickle young woman, her
unpretentious lover, and her forgiving husband, lately returned
from the war. The success of a play concerned with a triangular
relationship lies in piquing the audience to wonder which corner
will be eliminated. In the first place, Milne has made the lover so
shallow and pompous that there is never any doubt of the husband's victory. In the second place, he has made the heroine so
unappetizing that the victor is more to be pitied than envied.
Thus, the reduction of the triangle to a straight line offers nothing
more provocative than a problem in geometry solved on a black-
board. *The Stepmother,* the more serious and the more tolerable
of the two, concerns the wife of a highly respected Member of
Parliament and her accidental meeting with a young man who
has come to blackmail her husband. The young man, it seems, is
her husband's son by a mistress; word of his illegitimate birth
would, if publicized, wreck his father's career. At first he is glum
and embittered, but gradually the woman, his "stepmother" as

she identifies herself, soothes and mothers him into forgetting his threat.

All that *The Camberly Triangle* and *The Stepmother* tell us about Milne is that he did not always write well when he wrote briefly. Brevity is often the hallmark of his best work: his fairy-tale plays, in which the conversation approaches poetry and the characters, from the princess to the lowliest servant girl, make "once upon a time" seem yesterday, today, and tomorrow; his Pooh stories and Christopher Robin songs, in which every line is freighted with laughter or music. But the briefness of *The Camberly Triangle* and *The Stepmother* is paucity and not concentration; they present a gallery of waxworks—the Unfaithful Wife, the Other Man, the Bastard Son—which are slick, polished, and lifeless.

III   Three Plays

Milne remarks in his introduction to *Three Plays* (1923) that, unlike Shakespeare, he prefers to see his plays printed instead of acted; that to him as the author, "the part must always seem better than the player." Yet the fact that the second and third of these particular three plays so much as reached the stage is surely a tribute to the actors more than to Milne, for only the first deserves to be read, much less produced. *The Truth About Blayds* (performed in 1921), *The Dover Road* (in 1922), and *The Great Broxopp* (in 1923), the first good, the second passable, the third insipid, are a rapid descent from the heights of *Mr. Pim Passes By*. They are printed, however, exactly in reverse of the order in which they were written and produced. Milne's publishers may have recognized his decline and wished to obscure the chronological evidence.

The Truth About Blayds, which closes the volume and thus misleadingly appears to climax a three-year period in Milne's career, is the story of Oliver Blayds, a famous poet who, dying at the age of ninety, burdens his elder daughter, Isobel, with the confession that he has plagiarized most of his poems from the unpublished manuscripts of a dead friend. He has published them at carefully spaced intervals to maintain his reputation even into his dotage. Isobel is faced with a terrible decision. The family— her younger sister and the sister's husband and children—urges her to withhold the truth; in fact, it convinces itself that the dying

Blayds has imagined the whole deception, that the "dead friend" is a figment of senile fantasies. At least Isobel decides to follow the family's advice, not for its sake but for that of the poetry: a disillusioned public might well reject the poems along with the poet.

Milne admitted the difficulty of drawing a believable portrait of Blayds. "Now nothing is so difficult to put on the stage as a Great Man; and of all great men the most difficult to project across the footlights is the literary genius."[10] He approached the problem by indirection. First, he presented Blayds in the eyes of his family—to his grandchildren, fossilized but nonetheless formidable; to his daughters, a living god. Then he allowed the old man a brief, dignified appearance on stage in the company of a worshipful critic. Thus, off the stage or on, the Great Man dominates Act I. But Act II opens after his death, and critics declared that the play had died with Blayds. "I should have kept the old man alive," muttered Barrie.[11] Such a complaint is partially but not entirely justified. As Milne intended, *The Truth About Blayds* is not so much concerned with the man as with his effects on the members of his family, and he continues to affect them through the second and third acts. Though Milne intrudes a superfluous subplot to find Isobel a husband, he is always convincing with his more immediate materials, the deception and its consequences. The family who wants the truth withheld is made to seem money-minded rather than outright mercenary, insensitive rather than unprincipled; it is human and humanly fallible enough so that we can understand its viewpoint, even while we assure ourselves that we would have acted more nobly in the same circumstances, and Blayds himself, remembered after his death, remains a potent figure. Though he lied his way to fame, he grew in majesty to fit the position. He met and charmed both Swinburne and Tennyson, and he presented to public and critics the image of a Great Man. If not a major poet, he has been a magnificent impostor. Milne, himself a writer, conveys the literary scene with ease and conviction; and *The Truth About Blayds* is a play which, rarely less than good, disappoints only because it is not more often excellent.

The Dover Road is the story not of a poet but of a philanthropic gentleman, Mr. Latimer, whose spies alert him whenever a wife intends to desert her husband, or a husband his wife, to run away with a lover to live in sin. With the help of servants who appear to have learned their methods at Scotland Yard, he arranges to have the would-be sinners kidnapped and brought to his house on the Dover Road, where he forces them to spend a week in each other's continuous company and to reconsider their plans. Two couples are involved in the actual play: Leonard and his sweetheart, Anne; Leonard's wife Eustatia and *her* sweetheart, Nicholas. Eventually the men become so aggravated with the women that they drive off together to enjoy a womanless holiday in Cannes; unmarried Anne returns to her father; and Eustatia, who likes to play nurse, consoles herself by tending a feverish servant named Joseph.

Mr. Latimer is an appealing character, a kind of Anglicized Daddy Warbucks whose house possesses "an Arabian-night-adventure air," and whose psychological magic works a powerful spell. But the trouble with the play is the people involved in his spell: they are faceless whirligigs whom Mr. Latimer and the exigencies of the plot manipulate with such ease that they never seem more than paint and wood. In spite of Milne's contention that he would rather read his plays than see them performed on the stage, he has left the parts in *The Dover Road*, except for Mr. Latimer, so loosely defined that they demand the presence of actors and actresses to give them substance. It is possible to imagine, in Milne's day, the nondescript Anne assuming passion and beauty in the hands of a gifted actress, and Eustatia rendered humorous instead of simpering. But even a brilliant cast could not justify a revival. Modern audiences are considerably less fascinated with the problem of "living in sin" and "running away together" than Milne's Victorian-bred contemporaries; and his two couples, if they are going to occupy us for three long acts, must do considerably more than threaten to sleep together.

The Great Broxopp is the story of an advertising man who makes a fortune by giving his name to a baby's food and publicizing it under the slogan, "I am a Broxopp Baby—are you?" When his son, the first Broxopp baby, has grown to manhood and wishes to marry the daughter of a peer, Sir Roger Tenderden, Sir Roger insists that the name "Broxopp" has grown commercial and vulgar. Father and son must change their name; otherwise, marriage is out of the question. Sadly, Broxopp agrees to assume his wife's name of Chillingham and to retire from business. The children are duly married, but the smooth Sir Roger, to whom the renamed and retired Broxopp has entrusted his fortune, loses the last penny in foolish speculations. At the end of the play, the penniless Broxopp undertakes to promote a chicken feed under his new name (Chillingham's cheese for Chickens); and, this time helped by his son, he hopes to make the name as great—and as frankly commercial—as Broxopp.

The play is a blunt attack on snobbery and pretension. The hero is simple, unpretentious Broxopp; the villain, snobbish Sir Roger; and, caught between them, is a none too bright young man who almost becomes a snob but redeems himself when he breaks with his father-in-law and goes into business with his father. The playwright should be commended for his theme, but his simple man is a simpleton; his rich man, a stereotype; and their conflict is so obvious, the outcome so foreseeable, that it is hard to imagine even the versatile Edmund Gwenn as having animated the role of Broxopp. Perhaps in its time *The Great Broxopp* compensated for its papier-mâché characters by its revelation of modern advertising methods; but today, when alliterative and hyperbolic advertising slogans blare from road signs and television screens, it seems a dated period piece which is funny, if at all, for its clumsiness, not for its novelty.

IV　Four Plays

The *Four Plays* published in 1926 consist of three turgid and full-length disasters, *Success, Ariadne; or Business First,* and *To Have The Honour,* briefly redeemed by one small success, *Portrait of a Gentleman in Slippers,* which breasts the flood like a valiant Kon-Tiki in a Pacific of verbiage. The author has even omitted his customary introduction. Perhaps he felt that such plays did not deserve to be introduced. The same year saw the publication of *Winnie-the-Pooh,* and the public was treated and subjected to simultaneous views of a popular author at his best and worst.

Success, produced in 1923, concerns the fortunes of Selby Mannock, a "rising young Cabinet Minister in the late forties" who would rather become chancellor of the exchequer than prime minister. He is conveniently, if not ecstatically, married to Lady Jane, a woman "born in high politics" who has helped his career by entertaining the right people. But visiting a constituent by the name of Carchester, he encounters the wrong person, Mrs. Carchester, a childhood sweetheart whom he knew as Sally. Marriage, they decide, should be ecstatic instead of convenient; they will shed their respective mates and recover the rapture of their young love. Selby, knowing that a divorce will wreck his career, submits his resignation to the prime minister, who, however, misinterprets the gesture as a political ploy and offers to appoint him chancellor of the exchequer. The prize is irresistible. Selby sends a message to Sally: "I beg your pardon."

Success in its time was called a "problem play" and categorized with *Loyalties, Strife,* and *Justice* by John Galsworthy. But such plays, especially when named for abstractions, run the inevitable risk of subordinating the characters to their problems—of presenting plots which are no more than pulpits for delivering sermons. It is no doubt laudable for a dramatist to develop and display his social conscience, and Milne's era was one in which many dramatists, taking their cue from Ibsen and Shaw, were still concerned with equalizing the social inequalities and modernizing the moral provincialities of the nineteenth century. But the preacher should not eclipse the artist. Milne's sermon against false values, his plea that the highest success is won through love and not a career, is incontestible. But those who prefer a stage to a pulpit may justly reproach him for forgetting his proper function. Most of his characters appear to have stepped from the drawing room of Pinero's *The Second Mrs. Tanqueray,* and the conversations between Selby and Sally, intended to be idyllic, are unbelievable and saccharine.

To Have the Honour, produced in 1924 with Gerald Du Maurier as the prince, reads like a nineteenth-century operetta without music. Simon Battersby, an English gentleman of moderate means, and his daughter Angela, wistful, remote, imaginative, are preparing to give a party in their cottage at Wych Trentham for Prince Michael Robolosky of Neo-Slavonia, whom they have met on their recent holiday in southern France. Included among the guests is a certain Jennifer, a jolly young woman who claims to be the widow of a British army officer. But the Prince and Jennifer recognize each other at the party: he is not a prince, nor is she a widow; they are man and wife. Some years ago he had deserted her to become a soldier of fortune, and he had assumed various disguises. The bulk of the play is concerned with their on-again, off-again reconciliations. Jennifer, at least, is an unconventional heroine: she is thirty, plump, and endowed with a sense of humor which sometimes allows her to speak an amusing line. But the prince is the sort of man whom Tyrone Power played on innumerable stages and his son, in as many movies: a prettified, slim-hipped mannequin who is capable of two expressions, a grin and a grimace.

Ariadne; or Business First, produced in 1925, is predictable and predictably dull from the moment we read the opening stage directions: "The drawing-room of the Winters' house in Melchester." John Winter is money-minded more than wife-minded. He places his duties as a solicitor before his duties as a husband, and, when one of his clients, a handsome blackguard named Horace Meldrum, solicits his wife, Ariadne, he asks her to tolerate Horace for the sake of business. Ariadne does more than tolerate him; she pretends to fall in love with him and startles her husband into thinking of Ariadne first instead of business. Ariadne is Belinda reincarnated, as frivolous and as fatuous; and the men in her life are both such dullards that it is hard to choose between them. There are no memorable lines and no situations more original than the scene in which John, the outraged Victorian husband, shouts at Horace: "If I ever catch you in my house again, I'll thrash you within an inch of your life."

Portrait of a Gentleman in Slippers, the one small success in a book of large failures, is a closet drama rather than an acting piece. Its period is "once upon a time," and its chief characters are King Hilary XXIV and Princess Amaril, childhood sweethearts separated for many years but now engaged to be married. The outwardly noble and impressive king, who was once a bad little boy called Toto, now seems to his people the pattern for "all the kings that there have been in fairy-tales and history"; but he receives from a stranger the gift of a mirror, which shows him his true character: cruel, cowardly, deceitful, vain, cunning, and arrogant. In a moment of self-dramatization, he allows the princess to see him in the mirror. Surely, he thinks, she will wish to break their engagement. But the twisted image does not surprise her· it is what she has always loved. She cries joyfully to the mirror, "My ugly little, stupid little, vain little, bad little, *funny little* Toto!"

The action is slight, the characters few; the single scene is the king's chamber. It is a tiny tale but its tininess is that of a

Japanese netsuke, expertly carved from living wood. Milne, who strains in his modern plays to produce epigrams which will not appear strained, relaxes and seems at ease in his fairy tales. His words, unlabored, are quietly wise. For example, the stranger who brings the mirror says: "I have often noticed that the faults to which humble people most readily confess are those which, in less humble men, would be regarded as virtues." The typical fairy tales which we read as children—"Jack, the Giant-Killer" and "The Sleeping Beauty"—are naïve, obvious, and repetitious, but wonder redeems them from their narrative crudities. Milne has retained their wonder but added the needles of irony and the silks of discernment to make a fairy tale for adults.

For astute critics, if not yet for the public, *Four Plays* was an ominous volume in Milne's career as a dramatist. Greeted once as a bright, ascendant star, he was coming now to resemble a meteorite: brilliant for brief spaces but definitely falling. Meanwhile, a bear named Pooh, though his only flight had been on the end of a large balloon, was stocking his master's larder with honey jars for many a winter.

CHAPTER 3

The Falling Star

AFTER 1926, Milne's plays no longer appeared in collections. He had not forsaken the theater—not even Christopher Robin and Winnie-the-Pooh could keep him from his greatest love—but publishers were much more interested in collecting his children's poems and stories than his plays. Thus, in a sense, he was his own rival. Furthermore, his third and fourth collections of plays had shown the critics that Milne, the dramatist, was so comfortably ensconced in his drawing room that a dozen Freuds, a dozen Eugene O'Neills, could not dislodge him into the bold turbulence of modern drama. There was nothing wrong with his writing about drawing rooms; there was very much wrong with writing about them dully and to the exclusion of other subjects.

He still wrote plays, however; he still had occasional openings in New York and London. His more successful plays were published individually between hard covers; his less successful, or sometimes his shortest, in paperback acting editions. Notwithstanding their unevenness of quality and their range in length from one to four acts, it is possible to make some generalizations about them: his uncollected plays of the 1920's include his worst and also surprisingly some of his best work in the theater; his plays of the 1930's, consistently mediocre rather than good or bad, played, if at all, to unresponsive audiences and marked the decisive end of his vogue as a dramatist; his two subsequent plays, *The Ugly Duckling* in 1941 and *Before the Flood* in 1951, both of them brief, fanciful, and appealing, appeared too late and at too widely spaced intervals to recover a faded career.

I Of the 1920's

Two of Milne's plays were uncollected not because they were written after 1926 but because, though written in 1923, they did

51

CARNEGIE LIBRARY
LIVINGSTONE COLLEGE
c. 28144

not deserve collection even with such vacuities as *Ariadne* or *To Have the Honour*. *The Artist* is a one-act duologue in which an artist and a fickle young woman, coyly identified in the text as He and She, meet by chance in the cottage of a mutual friend, exchange insults, and fall in love because the Artist is unmethodical and the woman dislikes method. From the days of *Lovers in London*, Milne had been fond of such characters: a man and a woman whose courtship is a contest in absurdity; whose puns and wisecracks lead to a mocking proposal and a derisive acceptance. But the lovers in *The Artist*, like those in *Lovers in London*, are eminently unlovable because they deliver their japeries with the self-satisfied air of those who love their own cleverness more than each other.

The Man in the Bowler Hat: A Terribly Exciting Affair is a one-act play which concerns another he and she, though this time with names. John and Mary, a conventional and middle-aging couple, sit in their drawing room and yearn for excitement to alter their daily tedium. In answer to their wish, a man in a bowler hat invades the room and observes with silent detachment while a Hero and Heroine enter, withdraw, and reenter in the clutches of a Villain and a Bad Man, who threaten the Hero with torture unless he reveals the whereabouts of the Rajah's Ruby. The curtain falls with the Hero and Heroine unrescued and the ruby unrevealed. Only then are we told that we have watched the rehearsal for a first act, and the Man in the Bowler Hat is not a participant but a director. Though designed as a caricature of Victorian melodrama, the play is an undigested and indigestible fragment which cannot be excused by the author's protest that it is, after all, a rehearsal and not a finished production. In our present age, when rough drafts are produced, published, and dignified by the euphemism "Theatre of the Absurd," a term so vague that it could be applied to the gibberings in a cage of monkeys, no reader can be expected to exhume and enjoy such an effort from the 1920's—and certainly not from the works of a writer who, whatever his limitations, was capable of solid craftsmanship.

If *The Man in the Bowler Hat* is a spoof of Victorian melodrama, *The Perfect Alibi* (1928) is the kind of later melodrama which Ian Fleming has spoofed in his James Bond epics. Successfully produced on Broadway, and also in London as *The Fourth Wall*, *The Perfect Alibi* seems today a mystery without mysteriousness, as unoriginal as its title, and as unexciting as a Perry Mason story without a scene in court. Arthur Ludgrove is a retired English gentleman who spent his youth in South Africa and helped at one time to apprehend and convict three criminals. Two of the men, having served their terms in prison, come to England to exact revenge. No longer recognizable as Ludgrove knew them, they assume respectable identities, visit his country house as invited guests, and shoot their host in his study. Arranging the gun to suggest a suicide, they concoct a "perfect alibi" for the time of the murder. One of them claims to have been on the lake in a boat; and the other, a self-styled ornithologist, insists that he saw the boat through binoculars while looking for birds. But the victim's ward, clever young Susan, suspects the alibi for its very perfection—it is too convenient and tidy—and threatens one of the men until he confesses before a hidden witness.

There is no nicety of plot—from murder disguised as suicide to the forced confession before a concealed witness, which has not reappeared—and to better advantage—in later detective stories. And, except for a pair of police inspectors, one of them an aging local without suspicions, the other his brash and suspicious son from Scotland Yard, the characters seem contrived to fit the story, not to function as human beings. Even the clever heroine is the type of the Modern Girl who appears too often in Milne's plays and novels. Mystery writers should face the sad truth that plots, however ingenious, age like herring, but that good characters mellow like Provençal wines. It is Sherlock Holmes we remember, or Watson, that prince of listeners, and not the crimes they solve. Lacking a Sherlock or a Watson, *The Perfect Alibi* is rank with age and a little odorous.

Milne's next two plays, however, *The Ivory Door* and *Toad of Toad Hall*, are ageless instead of aged; both of them are fairy tales and both of them touched with the lightness, the sweetness, the wryness of Milne, the ironic dreamer. The first was published in January, 1929, and the author felt moved to claim that "It is the best play which I have written" and to chide the American critics who called it "whimsical" because it contained a magic door and a princess.[1] His critics, however, intended a compliment. Perversely charming, wryly amusing, exalted at times to wonder, the whimsy is not a weakness but a strength.

King Perivale, who is brave and handsome in the accepted style

of kings, is also curious; and curiosity leads him to speculate
about a certain door in his palace which, according to legend,
leads to death. No one who enters has ever been known to return.
The day of his wedding approaches; for reasons of state, he has
promised to marry a certain Princess Lilia, known to him only
through her official portrait. But how can he rule wisely—a wife
as well as a kingdom—if he balks at exploring a part of his own
palace? He enters the ivory door and finds not death, but a long,
dusty passage which soils his robes and leads him out of his
palace. Now, and not in the passage, his problems begin: no one
will readmit him to his own palace. True, his guards confess, he
looks like Perivale beneath his grime, but might he not be a
demon from behind the door who has stolen the king's body? The
princess arrives, ready to wed. When told that her promised
husband has disappeared through the door and that the man who
dirtily faces her is an arrant impostor, she is not convinced. "Show
me the door," she cries, and follows the route of the king. Emerg-
ing, she looks like a chimney sweep. "Demon!" the people shout,
and they threaten to kill her along with Perivale. But the superstitious courtiers, suspecting more demons behind the door and
fearing their wrath, order the king and the princess to rejoin and
pacify them. Hand in hand, Perivale and Lilia open the ivory
door and walk to freedom in the great, unshackled world.

Like most fairy tales, the play has a point: that people demand
illusions. Perivale's subjects would rather lose their king than
their superstitions about the door—a theme Eugene O'Neill was
to illustrate differently but no more compellingly in *The Iceman
Cometh*. Milne makes a further point: that the rare man who can
live without legends, without self-deception, may lose a throne
but gain the inestimable prize of self-fulfillment. And he says
these things not through painted puppets, but through a king who
is also a man and a princess who is more than beautiful, and
through speeches believably conversational yet chiseled as carefully as if they were blank verse and inlaid with wisdom as well
as wit.

The Ivory Door was followed in April of the same year by *Toad
of Toad Hall;* and the sequence, intentional or accidental, is inspired. It is almost as if the forest of Mr. Toad and his friends is
the world which lies beyond the ivory door: a wonderland entered
through magic portals. Milne was an earnest admirer of Kenneth

Grahame's *The Wind in the Willows,* the book which inspired his play. In *Not That It Matters,* Milne described it as a "book which everybody in the household loves and quotes continually ever afterwards; a book which is read aloud to every new guest, and is regarded as the touchstone of his worth. . . . Well, of course, you will order the book at once. But I must give you one word of warning. When you sit down to it, don't be so ridiculous as to suppose that you are sitting in judgment on my taste, still less on the genius of Kenneth Grahame. You are merely sitting in judgment on yourself. . . . You may be worthy; I do not know. But it is you who are on trial."[2] In a later essay, "Mr. Grahame, Mr. Roosevelt, and I," he takes credit with Theodore Roosevelt for having rescued *The Wind in the Willows* from oblivion and adds: "The young man gives it to the girl with whom he is in love, and if she does not like it, asks her to return his letters. The older man tries it on his nephew, and alters his will accordingly."[3]

Milne put himself on trial when he tried to adapt a series of loosely joined, delicately lyrical episodes to meet the harsh requirements of the modern stage. He resembled Grahame to the point that the same artist, Ernest Shepard, could illustrate *Winnie-the-Pooh* and *The Wind in the Willows;* but he also differed from him. Grahame is more often wistful than whimsical. There is more of terror in him and more of that piercing beauty which, to borrow Tennyson's phrase, rises from the "depth of some divine despair." Milne, who recognized their differences, frankly admitted his inability to recapture the lyricism of such a chapter as "The Piper at the Gates of Dawn." He only attempted to preserve the comedy; but, in spite of his modest aim, he produced an adaptation which was also a work of art. To Grahame's original humor he added the sly hilarity which had carried Pooh in search of the North Pole and to trap a Heffalump. *Toad of Toad Hall* is slighter—in size as well as in scope—than *The Wind in the Willows,* but also merrier; it is a romp instead of a pastoral.

Because of the theatrical conventions of Milne's day, which required a recognizable plot with ascending action, a climax, and a denouement—in short, a "well-made play"—he has concentrated on the ludicrous Mr. Toad, his mania for motor cars, his imprisonment, his escape, and his recapture of Toad Hall from the squatters who have occupied it during his absence. He has necessarily reduced Rat, Badger, and Mole to the status of prominent subordinates and omitted such charming but extraneous episodes as the visit of the Sea Rat and the piping of Pan at the Gates of Dawn. But Milne's additions are more admirable than his subtractions are regrettable.

In Grahame, there is a horse, unnamed and inarticulate, who pulls Toad's gypsy caravan. In Milne, the horse is named Alfred and is richly characterized as an erudite conversationalist who does not object to pulling a wagon so long as his passengers are good listeners, and who loves to flaunt such words as "anticyclonic disturbance" and "cataclysm." In Grahame, Mr. Toad is sentenced to jail in the space of a page, but Milne expands his trial to a rollicking scene of twelve pages. Charges are hurled and denied of automobile theft, reckless driving, and sassing an officer. Mr. Toad's friends—Alfred, Rat, Mole, and Badger—rush to defend him. Mr. Toad's enemies, the weasels, rush to accuse him, and one of them tries to pass for an innocent rabbit out of pure devilment. Finally, Milne has added a sprinkling of songs to those supplied by Grahame; and, being a better light versifier, he has even managed to make the disreputable Wild Wooders sing with the lilt of Christopher Robin (though a somewhat devilish lilt), as when they plot the downfall of Toad: "Day and night the elder Weasels *Hope* that he will have the measles. . . ."

Unaccountably, Milne has superimposed a framework in which a little girl, Marigold, who is visiting a riverbank with her nurse, appears to be dreaming the action of the animals. Perhaps he wished to attract sophisticated adults as well as credulous children and felt that they needed some preparation before they could accept the reality of Toad, Rat, Mole, and Badger on the stage; they needed a child to coax them through the looking glass. As he wrote in his introduction, "There is a horrid realism about the theatre, from which, however hard we try, we can never quite escape." But he underestimated the compulsion of the characters created by Grahame and re-created by himself. Once they possess the stage, only an incorrigible realist could fail to believe in them. Toad behind the wheel of his new motor car, drunk with speed; Rat, asking nothing more of life than to mess about "by a river—or *in* a river—or *on* a river"; young, impulsive Mole, who, Milne suggested "might well be played by some boyish young actress"; and staunch old Badger, a little crotchety, a little stern at times, but always on hand when the Wild Wooders threaten their mischief.

We have all seen them, of course, in their human counterparts. Why then show them as beasts? Because the distortion which is fantasy—in this case the addition of fur, feathers, and inimitable charm to human characteristics—is a way of showing old truths in a new light, in the illuminating flash of recognition which fathers understanding. The truth of Toad and company, both Grahame's and Milne's, is that men are often foolish; they scheme and quarrel and fight; but some of them also are loving friends and vessels of awe and merriment.

Toad of Toad Hall, like most adaptations, unavoidably stirred the wrath of those who believe that fine novels cannot become equally fine plays; that adapting means diminishing. Grahame's biographer, Peter Green, dismissed Milne's effort as "mere sentimental cosiness."⁴ But Grahame and his wife, who shared a box with Milne when *Toad of Toad Hall* opened in London, nodded their heads and smiled in silent approval. Time has confirmed their verdict. For many years the play was revived for the Christmas holidays; presented by the Liverpool Repertory Theatre in 1957, it gave the rising young actress, Rita Tushingham, her first stage role as the rear end of a donkey; and now, no longer shown on the stage, it prospers in a handsome new edition for young readers (1965).

The journey from *Toad of Toad Hall* to *Michael and Mary* is as unwelcome as the return of the Darling children from Never-Never Land. *Michael and Mary,* first produced in 1929 with Herbert Marshall and Edna Best in the title roles and first published in 1931, is the story of poor but ambitious young man who meets and befriends a girl in the British Museum. Her husband, it seems, has left the country and deserted his wife without support. Michael finds her a room in his apartment house and, unable to locate the husband, illegally marries her. Thirteen years elapse between acts, and Michael reappears as a highly successful writer who lives with the still beautiful Mary and their son David in prosperous lodgings at Chelsea. But Mary's first husband, Harry Price by name, returns from America to threaten the couple with blackmail: unless they agree to his price, he will tell the authorities about their bigamous marriage.

When the outraged Michael shoves him toward the door, Price collapses and dies of a heart attack. Michael, however, invents a story to tell the police: Price was a total stranger who read his

name in the papers, came to beg money, and died of natural
causes. The police (if not the audience) accept the story, and
Michael and Mary enjoy between acts a decade of happy marriage and reappear in the final act with their son David and their
new daughter-in-law, Romo. It is time, they feel, to confess their
deception to the children and ask forgiveness; they confess and
receive the children's wholehearted admiration. But the police,
who have finally learned the truth, are less forgiving. When the
curtain falls, Michael must serve a short prison term for conceal-
ing the real nature of Price's death.

Critics accused Milne of sentimentality in his portrait of
Michael and Mary, and their dutiful son, who seizes and kisses
their hands when they confess their bigamy. But the fault of the
play lies less in sentimentality than in awkward and often laughable melodrama. The villainous husband who suffers a convenient
heart attack—the writer-hero devising his alibi as he strides,
soliloquizing, across the stage—are gimmicks as old as the melodrama of the nineteenth century, as old as the creaking thrillers
of Dion Boucicault, father of that same Dion who produced
Belinda and *Mr. Pim Passes By.* Milne himself had reservations
about the scene of the alibi; his American producer told him that
"the New York *Michael* attacked that scene in thirty different
ways at their long-continued rehearsals, before a thirty-first way
was discovered which carried the audience."[5] All in all, *Michael
and Mary* is an earnest, thoughtful, and well-intentioned failure,
an inoffensive but disappointing return from the mansion of Mr.
Toad and the boon companionship of Mole, Rat, and Badger.

II   *Of the 1930's*

Milne's four plays of the 1930's, *Other People's Lives, Miss
Marlowe at Play, Miss Elizabeth Bennett,* and *Sarah Simple,* were
the valiant but pathetic efforts of a dramatist who had yet to recognize that his gift for drama, sporadic at best, had dwindled into
mere technical competence. Celebrated, even adulated, for *Winnie-the-Pooh,* he could not quite be ignored by producers, who
still gave him major productions in London and New York, or by
audiences, who still attended his openings with the wistful hope
that they would see another *Toad of Toad Hall.* To critics, however, Milne seemed an anachronism from the 1920's, who, over-

rated even at his peak, was now so negligible that he could be ignored.

Other People's Lives, first presented in 1933 and first published in 1935, at least attempted some characters new to Milne: young people who were not merely brash and modern like the young sweethearts in *Mr. Pim Passes By*, but sophisticated to the point of malice; people whose satiric darts seemed dipped in curare and who faintly foreshadowed the damned and damning quartet in Edward Albee's *Who's Afraid of Virginia Woolf?* Milne's Arnold and Lola Waited are worldly and well-to-do intellectuals who have taken a "lower middle class apartment" to indulge a penchant for slumming. They are often visited by Stephen Bellerby, a young publisher, and his wife Mary, whose outward heartiness conceals an inward heartlessness. With the exception of Lola, who is subject to infrequent scruples, the four of them are thoroughly detestable. At the same time, they are dramatically vibrant. They repel us but they compel us. "What the Proust do you care?" swears Arnold, and shaft follows shaft with lethal, even if somewhat literary, precision. Such characters, developed throughout the play, might have earned for Milne at least a gallery seat in the living, maturing theater of the 1930's.

But the four sophisticates soon become bored with one another; they want new games, new objects of condescension and ridicule. They decide to dabble in "other people's lives," and the other people they choose, the Trillings, are so poor and deserving—the mother, a hopeless cripple; the father, a working man who aspires to be a novelist; the daughter, a paragon of filial obedience—that they appear to have stepped from the panels of "Little Orphan Annie." In the Trillings, Milne intended a kindly contrast to his intellectuals; he attained caricatures.

As the dullest playgoer can predict, when the overprivileged adopt the underprivileged out of boredom and not humanity, the adoption must lead to misfortune. Stephen Bellerby promises to consider Mr. Trilling's novel for his publishing house. After chuckling over its ineptitudes with his wife, he loses the manuscript and blandly reports the loss to Trilling as if he were apologizing for a misplaced magazine. But there are still ways to "improve" the Trillings. Together, the Waites and the Bellerbys arrange for the daughter to visit Canada and for Mrs. Trilling to have an operation to correct her lameness. No sooner has the daughter left the country than the mother dies in the hospital. Are the Waites and the Bellerbys sorry? Lola suffers one of her scruples, but the general feeling is: "Well, this project failed us. Let's find another." Herein lies the failure of the play: the extreme callousness of the do-gooders is not extremely shocking, since the objects of their perverted good are too saccharine to earn our sympathy.

In *Other People's Lives*, Milne had written a drama with something to say, even if he had said it well only when he wrote with unaccustomed venom. In his next play, he undertook a farce whose one object was to amuse. *Miss Marlowe at Play* (1936) is a "one-act Comedy" about a famous and happily married actress who is accused by an irate father, Ambrose Wallington, of having seduced his son. She is innocent; she is outraged; and she decides to play with her accuser. She lures him to her apartment and arranges for her husband, alerted to the plot, to fling open the door, pretend surprise, and thunder accusations. Wallington is cowed and chagrined, and the audience is equally chagrined that a seasoned playwright should imagine he has written a play, when he has simply decorated an anecdote which, elaborated for the stage, framed and spotlighted, is not so much playful as painful.

The 1930's, it seemed, were not to be propitious for Milne: he had failed with a serious drama; he had failed with a farce. Nothing remained for him except to return to the form which had made his name, a comedy of manners. With little to lose and with a lost career to regain, he reached to the heights for his subject. In *Miss Elizabeth Bennett* (1936), he chose to dramatize Jane Austen's *Pride and Prejudice*. After all, he had successfully dramatized Grahame's *The Wind in the Willows*, and he felt as much at ease in Jane Austen's nineteenth-century country houses as he did in the hall of Mr. Toad.

He admitted that such an adaptation was the "most difficult and the most delightful" of all the "damnably difficult and delightful things to try to do."[6] He borrowed the best passages of dialogue directly from the novel and tried to embed them in his own words without a perceptible break. He tried to enliven the somewhat wooden Darcy with an "ironic tang." He tried to make the play intelligible even to those who had never read *Pride and Prejudice*. In all three attempts he succeeded. The borrowed passages do not obtrude; Darcy is improved as a man if not as a character; and those unfamiliar with the novel can follow the play without confusion.

But Milne has lost much more than he has retained or gained. His heroine—she for whom he named his play and whom, unlike Miss Austen, he emphasized at the expense of all other characters —is a shadowy resurrection and not a re-creation. The witty, resourceful, and altogether enchanting Elizabeth of the novel remains witty and resourceful but no longer enchanting. Jane Austen used description as well as dialogue to limn her heroine; in a phrase, a line, or a paragraph, she etched a portrait with the concision and assurance of a master miniaturist. Milne has only dialogue to serve his purpose. His problem is that of all playwrights who hope to transpose a novel to the stage: they cannot interpret the characters for their audience; they can only let them speak and be interpreted. In the case of a beloved classic like *Pride and Prejudice*, Milne's problem was monumental, since lovers of the book would come to the play with a preconception and a demand: a preconceived Elizabeth and the demand that any playwright presumptuous enough to borrow her must preserve, if not improve, her. Milne's articulate shadow speaks, postures, laughs on the stage; momentarily amuses and enlightens; but fades from the mind as soon as she fades from view. The Elizabeth Bennett who defies forgetfulness belongs to Jane Austen.

Sarah Simple—first performed in 1937, first published in 1939— reverts to the farce of *Miss Marlow at Play* and, in effect, confesses the author's dramatic bankruptcy. The ease of the dialogue cannot conceal the inanity of the characters and the foolishness which passes for a plot. Milne often attempted and never wrote a successful farce. He tried too hard; his characters try too hard. Their gibes are as grating as the cackles from a television laugh machine. William Bendish, a thirty-six-year-old dilettante who dabbles with inventions but prefers to vegetate, becomes infatuated with Marianne Bell-Mason, a portly but comely widow of a deceased canon. Their plans to wed, however, are thwarted by the return of William's wife, who had run off with a lover some eight years ago and whom William had neglected to divorce. She had taken the professional name of Sarah Simple and became a hat designer in America. The reconciliation of William and wife might properly have occupied one act, but Milne has protracted his minimal action into three acts by intruding an absolutely pointless nephew and niece and by forsaking his story line to pursue puns and attempt epigrams.

To the critics, *Sarah Simple* confirmed their suspicion that they no longer needed to damn Milne's plays; they could dismiss them. Why concern themselves with *Other People's Lives* when Emlyn Williams had shown in *The Corn Is Green* that the working classes could be sympathetically portrayed even if they were unsentimentalized? Why endure the diminishment which was *Miss Elizabeth Bennett* when Eugene O'Neill had shown in *Mourning Becomes Electra* that classics far older than *Pride and Prejudice* could be restated and revitalized for the modern stage? Milne himself blamed Pooh for overshadowing his later plays. But Pooh was blameless. Throughout the 1930's, Milne produced nothing to overshadow.

III   *Of the 1940's and 1950's*

During the 1940's Milne occupied himself first with his war pamphlets, then with his novel *Chloe Marr* and the stories collected in *Birthday Party* and *A Table Near the Band*. He had not so much lost his interest in the theater as lost his audience, which, nurtured on Freud and Jung, Eliot and Pound, Lenin and Stalin, had deserted him during the 1930's for the urgent timeliness of Maxwell Anderson's *Winterset* and Robert Sherwood's *The Petrified Forest*. When the 1940's arrived to launch the careers of Tennessee Williams and Arthur Miller, Milne as a dramatist was remembered if at all for *Mr. Pim Passes By*, anthologized in Bennett Cerf's *Sixteen Famous British Plays;* and those who rode the Williams had shown in *The Corn Is Green* that the working classes *and Mary* as a heavy-handed parody or laughed it off the stage.

Milne did not write to please an audience. On the other hand, he did not like to write plays which were unpublishable or unproduceable when he could occupy his pen with other and more acceptable projects and at the same time extend the dimensions of his diversified career. Throughout the entire 1940's, he wrote a single play, the one-act *Ugly Duckling* (1941); and he wisely chose for his characters not the aristocrats of his drawing-room comedies, the ghosts of a faded era, but the fadeless king and

queen "of any country from any story-book," and their unmarried
daughter, the Princess Camilla—unmarriageable because she is
ugly, though "quite the nicest person in the Kingdom." Many a
prince has vied for her hand from a distance, seen her face, and
left the country by the first steed or, lacking a steed, drowned
himself in the moat. The good of the kingdom, however, as well
as the conventions of a fairy tale, require a husband for every
princess; and the King and Queen decide on a desperate stratagem. They invite a certain Prince Simon a wanderer in foreign
lands, to court their daughter. But they plan to present him on his
arrival with the pretty waiting maid Dulcibella; introduce her as
the princess; and, once he is snared, marry him to the real princess who is to be disguised behind a veil. What they do not suspect is that Simon, likable but unromantically plain, intends a
similar stratagem. His handsome attendant Carol is to present
himself as the Prince and presumably captivate the Princess; but
Simon, disguised in armor, is to marry her.

Simon, however, arrives ahead of schedule, meets Camilla instead of Dulcibella, and finds her beautiful. Thanks to her fairy
godmother, it seems, she enjoys the questionable gift of appearing
ugly to everyone except her bethrothed until her wedding day;
thus, she is spared the compliments which turn a young girl's
head and make her proud and selfish. As for Simon, his looks are
not illusory; he is quite the plainest of princes. But Camilla values
the man and not his looks. They confess their identical schemes
and fall in love. On her wedding day, the King appraises his
daughter with a quizzical eye. To the queen he says: "My dear,
have we been wrong about Camilla all this time? It seemed to me
that she wasn't looking quite so plain as usual just now. Did *you*
notice anything?"

The Ugly Duckling, like *Portrait of a Gentleman in Slippers*, is
a graceful closet drama whose speeches are so delicately and yet
so forcefully wrought, whose characters are so gossamer and yet
so sensible, that no modern stage could quite encompass their
magic. For such a play, the mind is the best theater. Secure in the
pages of *Twenty-Four Favorite One-Act Plays*, it glides like a
shapely swan among the powerful predators of Eugene O'Neill,
Tennessee Williams, and Arthur Miller.

A full decade elapsed between *The Ugly Duckling* and Milne's
final play, *Before the Flood*, which grew from a short story pub-

lished in *A Table Near the Band.* For his method if not for his
characters, he looked to John Erskine, whose novel *Private Life
of Helen of Troy* was one of the books which, Milne once remarked, he would most have liked to write. Like Erskine, he takes
an irreverent look at history. In Homer, Helen is remote and
majestic; in Erskine, she is brash, chic, and sophisticated. In the
Bible, Noah is a lordly patriarch; in Milne, he is a funny old
gentleman who interprets his nightmares as prophecies from
Yahweh. When he dreams that a flood will engulf the world, his
family humors him and agrees to help with the ark; but his wife
Hannah remarks: "You really do believe it? You know, dear,
sometimes your prophecies—there was that one the other day that
Ham was going to be eaten by a lion. . . ." Says Noah: "If you
remember, Hannah, Ayesha had an unaccountable illness shortly
afterwards, which is exactly what the grief and shock would have
caused if Ham *had* been eaten by a lion." At the end of the play,
Hannah looks at the sky, holds out a hand, and cries: "It's
raining!" Since Erskine and Milne are both teasers instead of de-
bunkers, since they like their subjects even while they banter
them, Helen without her sorrows is not without her charms, and
Noah has lost his dignity but not his humanity.

Again like Erskine, Milne is a teacher as well as a tease. Helen,
though playful, is nobody's fool; and the men in her life, who
seem to have made her their pawn, have underestimated the
power of her allurements. Noah, the foolish dreamer, does not
look ridiculous when the rains begin to fall; and his sons Ham
and Shem have been treated seriously throughout the play in their
relationship with their wives, Ayesha and Kerin. Ham and
Ayesha, for example, believe that they have fallen out of love
when they have merely fallen into silence. They must learn to forget pride and admit affection:

Ham. I used to watch your face in the mirror. So lovely; so far away,
    in some quiet world of your own.
Ayesha. I don't think you ever told me.
Ham. I thought you knew.
Ayesha. Don't ever think that of me. Never think that I know.[7]

But Erskine allows himself the scope of a full-length novel in
which to teach and to tease, while Milne has limited himself to a
one-act play. There are times when his jokes, however amusing,
and his insights, however resourceful, seem as rudely juxtaposed,

as ill at ease with each other, as the animals crowded into the ark. *Before the Flood* is a good but slight and imperfect play. It is hardly fair to ask perfection of an aging and out-of-practice playwright. Still, it is hard to read about Noah without nostalgia for Mr. Pim, that earlier and much more remarkable elderly eccentric, and without regret that the "bright Aldebaran" of modern drama should end as a firefly instead of a star.

CHAPTER 4

A House for Many Summers

A House for Many Summers

ONCE ON A TIME, written and published during World War I (1917), has been the outcast of Milne's juveniles, a stepchild among those legitimate and honored children, *When We Were Very Young, Now We Are Six, Winnie-the-Pooh,* and *The House at Pooh Corner*. The book has always been hard to classify. Milne himself insisted that he wrote it not for children but for grown-ups, and "more particularly for two grown-ups. My wife and myself. . . ."[1] As a novel for adults, it appeared at the outset of his career as a dramatist, when author and public were more concerned with his plays. Revived in the 1920's as a children's book, it was overshadowed by Pooh and Christopher Robin and, like a bad child, relegated to the attic. But in 1962 a wise American publisher recognized that *Once on a Time* need not be limited to any particular age and produced a new edition, packaged in pink and jauntily illustrated, for children "10 and up and up and up."

Said Milne of writing the book with his wife Daphne on the Isle of Wight: "it was the greatest fun to do. We began every evening at half-past five, I in my chair before the fire, my collaborator, pen in hand, brown head bent over table, writing, waiting, laughing: it made the war seem very far away, it took us back to our own happy life in London."[2] The story is woven from familiar but unfaded threads, as bright as gold from the loom of Rumpelstiltskin or the tresses of Rapunzel. While Merriwig, king of Euralia, is breakfasting with his daughter Hyacinth, the king of adjacent Barodia flies over the palace in his seven-league boots and, flaunting his ginger whiskers, distracts the eye and spoils the appetite of the royal breakfasters. Incensed, Merriwig orders his archers to clear the sky under the pretext of target practice, and one of them manages to bend a trailing whisker. The aerial king returns to Barodia to fire a stiff note of protest, receives a mocking reply, and declares war on Euralia. Promptly Merriwig invades Barodia and leaves his kingdom in the hands of Hyacinth.

But Hyacinth is an inexperienced seventeen, and her one dependable friend is a little girl named Wiggs, who owns a wishing ring given to her by a fairy. In the king's absence, the unscrupulous Countess Belvane, an epic poetess when she is not conniving to rule the country or confessing unbridled ambitions to her diary, usurps power from the princess. Desperate, Hyacinth dispatches a messenger to Prince Udo of Araby and asks for his help. Accompanied by a friend named Coronel, a young man as staunch and sensible as Udo is foolish and foppish, Udo hurries to her assistance; but Belvane, with the help of the wishing ring which she steals from Wiggs, bewitches Udo into an animal of indeterminate species: "He had the mane and the tail of a lion. In between the tail and the mane it is difficult to say what he was, save that there was an impression of magnificence about his person—such magnificence, anyhow, as is given by an astrakhan-trimmed fur coat."

In his mongrelized state, Udo proves a poor ally for hapless Hyacinth. He slouches about the palace and nibbles watercress sandwiches. Only with the help of Wiggs, who recovers her wishing ring from Belvane, does he regain his original shape and prepare to help and possibly to woo the princess. By this time, however, Hyacinth has fallen in love with Coronel; and Belvane decides that she herself will marry Udo, so recently the object of her sorceries, and go to rule with him in Araby. But when King Merriwig suddenly wins his war against Barodia and returns in triumph, brandishing the whiskers of his defeated enemy, Belvane decides that she would rather marry a returning king than a departing prince. Friendless and wifeless, but relieved to be rid of the ambitious Belvane, Udo departs for Araby. Belvane writes in her diary "Became good" and marries the king, while Hyacinth and Coronel are married in the same ceremony.

"This is a Fairy Story," wrote Milne, "and it is a Fairy Story for grown-ups because I have tried to give some character to the people who wander through its pages. Children prefer incident to character; if character is to be drawn, it must be done broadly, in tar or whitewash. Read the old fairy stories and you will see with what simplicity, with what perfection of method, the child's needs are met. Yet there must have been more in Fairyland than that. . . ."[3]

Certainly there is more in Milne's Fairyland. The princess in most such tales is young, golden-haired, virtuous, and vapid; she is a type, in fact a stereotype, an excuse for the prince to slay dragons and utter protestations of love, and scarcely more human than a wax madonna. The prince is her masculine counterpart, handsome, valiant, and vacant. He wields a mighty sword; he woos with pretty speeches; but, when he is said to live happily ever afterward with the princess, it is hard to imagine how they will spend their time. So wooden and featureless are the conventional fairy-tale lovers that a motion picture producer like Walt Disney, when he animates *Cinderella* or *Snow White*, must surround them with dwarfs or animals which, paradoxically, are far more human than the humans whom they befriend. Milne's lovers, on the other hand, exist and enchant in their own right. The princess is an uncomplicated and plausible young girl who finds herself overshadowed and victimized by a mature and beautiful woman: "Belvane had always a curious effect on the Princess when they were alone together. There was something about her large manner which made Hyacinth feel like a schoolgirl who has been behaving badly: alarmed and apologetic." Because she has human weaknesses, she wins our commiseration; because she has human resourcefulness, she wins our admiration.

Hyacinth finds an ideal suitor in Coronel, who, though less than a prince, is at least a duke in the court of Prince Udo. Instead of slaying dragons and rescuing damsels, he must dance attendance on Udo; praise him to the ladies; and, in the way of Anna with the king of Siam, feed him questions which will allow Udo to shine as a conversationalist. He is a hero who, throughout the story, is allowed no duel with which to prove his heroism, neither walls to scale nor dragons to slay. But the forest idyll in which he meets the princess reveals him as more than a hero: as a young man with whom Hyacinth may indeed expect to live happily ever after the wedding.

Such engaging lovers deserve a formidable adversary, one as carefully characterized as themselves, and one quite naughty enough to give them a book full of troubles. They find her in Belvane. When she first appears in the story, the king asks her:

"What *were* we talking about yesterday?" " 'Oh, your Majesty,'
said the Countess, 'affairs of state,' and she gave him that wicked,
innocent, impudent, and entirely scandalous look which he never
could resist, and you couldn't either, for that matter."[4] She casts a
magic spell when she metamorphoses Udo, but her spells are not
dependent on wishing rings. Her wit and beauty enable her to
accomplish more than any mere ring: to make a king feel kingly,
a prince princely, and the king's subjects governed rather than
subjected. (In one of the asides permitted to the author of a fairy
tale, Milne confesses that he has met her, reincarnated, in an
English country house.)

Even Belvane's wickedness commands our respect. She initiates
a poetry contest in the realm and awards the prize to herself for
an epic written under the assumed name of Charlotte Patacake
and containing the immortal lines: "Five hundred men behind
him marched to fight—"Left-right, left-right, left-right, left-right,
left-right.' "[5] Furthermore, she drains the money from the treasury
under the pretext of financing an army of Amazons, actually non-
existent, and redistributes the gold to the populace in order to
win their cheers. And we have this revealing extract from her
diary:

> *Monday,* June first. Became bad.
> *Tuesday,* June second. Realized in the privacy of my heart that I
> was destined to rule the country.
> *Wednesday,* June third. Decided to oust the princess.
> *Thursday,* June fourth. Began ousting.[6]

On the strength of such full-bodied and full-blooded characters
as Hyacinth, Coronel, and Belvane, Milne has achieved his fairy
tale for adults. At the same time, consciously or not, he has written for children. Despite satiric flashes, his book is not a satire. It
is neither a parody nor a spoof. It does not disturb a child with
the vague suspicion that someone is "pulling his leg." Modern
fiction is rife with adult fairy tales which tell old-fashioned adventures in order to satirize or allegorize modern events and morals.
Orwell's *Animal Farm* is not primarily a tale of talking pigs and
sheep, but a satire about acquisitive dictators and the sheeplike
people to whom they dictate. Isak Dinesen's *The Angelic Aveng-
ers,* published in occupied Denmark during World War II, is not
primarily a romance about two young girls threatened by a vil-

lainous lord and defended by a voodoo priestess, but an allegory
aimed at glorifying the Danes and vilifying the Germans. But
Milne's *Once on a Time* is a story without a lesson, much less a
moral, a tale told to amuse and not to teach.

As Milne recognized in his Foreword, children do not concern
themselves with the niceties of characterization. They love the
rush of his incidents, the seven-league boots, the war with
Barodia, the transformation of Udo; and the characters live for
them only insofar as they participate in droll or exciting adventures. They hiss Belvane in the midst of her machinations, much
as they hiss the stepmother in *Snow White;* and they fail to
appreciate the imaginativeness of her villainies. They cheer the
young lovers for their schemes to outwit Belvane, but miss the
lyricism of their tryst in the forest. Best of all, they like the misadventures of Prince Udo after Belvane has wished him into a
lion-sheep-rabbit, but they overlook the wry, sly humor of his
dialogue, for example, in the scene where he wonders if he will
need to hibernate:

> Udo was decidedly embarrassed. He wriggled. He drew little circles
> with his hind paw on the ground and he shot little coy glances at her.
> "Well, I"—and he gave a little nervous giggle—"I have a sort of
> uneasy feeling that I may be one of those animals"—he gave another
> conscious little laugh—"that have to go to sleep all through the winter.
> It would be very annoying if I"—his paw became very busy here—"if
> I had to dig a little hole in the ground, just when the plot was
> thickening."
> "Oh, but you won't," said Hyacinth, in distress.
> They were both silent for a moment, thinking of the awful possi-
> bilities. Udo's tail had fallen across Hyacinth's lap, and she began to
> play with it absently.
> "Anyway," she said hopefully, "it's only July now."[7]

Thanks to such lively scenes and others like them, agreeable to
children and parents for different reasons, *Once on a Time* suggests comparison to T. H. White's *The Sword in the Stone*, which,
though published twenty-two years after Milne's book, has already achieved the status which *Once on a Time* deserves: that
of a recognized classic in juvenile literature. Both stories are light-
hearted adventures laid in medieval countries, with moated
castles, jousting knights, and enchanted forests at every turn of a
page. Both contain a man or a boy who is turned by spells into

animals—in Milne, Udo becomes three animals at once; in White, the young Arthur, nicknamed Wart, becomes a bird, a fish, a snake, and a hedgehog, though not at the same time—and both contain enchantresses who are wily, beautiful, and thirty years old.

But the books in other ways are profoundly different. If *Once on a Time* is for "10 and up and up and up," then *The Sword in the Stone* is for "12 and up and up and up." White's book is longer and more ambitious. In part, he achieves his humor by giving a detailed and accurate description of a castle, a forest, a duel, and then intruding a deliberate and glaring anachronism. In a thirteenth-century English landscape, we are suddenly confronted by *Encyclopaedia Britannicas*, electricity, and *Morning Posts*. Wart, who is searching for the wicked fairy, Morgan Le Fay, passes through a forest which White describes to the last tree, the last bird, the last sound—a forest so real, old, and English that the swish of the book's pages seems the rustle of wind in leaves or the flight of an aery-mouse leaping from branch to branch. But, when Wart confronts the castle of Morgan Le Fay, he finds a neon sign emblazoned like the marquee of a theater: "The Queen of Air and Darkness, Now Showing." The queen herself is a "very beautiful lady, wearing beach pajamas and smoked glasses. One side of her yellow hair fell over the right optic of her glasses, and she was smoking a cigarette in a long green jade holder as she lay full length on a white leather sofa."

Milne, however, once he has entered fairyland, never violates its established boundaries. He may speak an aside as the author of the book; but—within his story, within the kingdoms of Araby, Euralia, and Barodia—he allows no intrusion from the modern, workaday world. His enchantress, Belvane, does not disport herself in beach pajamas and dark glasses, and his castle is not equipped with electricity or neon signs. Writing *Once on a Time* in the midst of a world war which threatened his life as well as his way of life, he felt the need for a past without reminders of the disagreeable present.

Milne does not, it is true, attempt to be *specifically* medieval, in the way of White describing the castle of Sir Ector. His scenes, far from detailed, are as pleasant and vague as his title, "Once on a Time"—which time? We are given no hint except for the knights and castles. With a few agile strokes, Milne sketches a broad scene which the reader must furnish with details from his own imaginings and his own experience. His forest is not composed of oaks, beeches, and elms; it is simply a forest with an "open glade," a "gurgling brook," and a "soft green yonder." His castle consists of towers and battlements, and not, like White's, of barbicans, bartizans, portcullises, bosses, and shell-keeps. White has aimed at particularity, whether in medievalism or anachronism; Milne has aimed at the general, not the particular, but within his generality he maintains the unbroken aura of fairyland.

If Milne suggests comparison to White, he demands comparison to Barrie. Both Milne and Barrie, as readers reminded them until they winced at the word, excelled at whimsy. Critics have sometimes grumbled that both men waxed excessively whimsical in their plays for adults, not only in dialogue but in stage directions. But in their children's stories, whimsy is always at home, since a child's world is compounded less of sense than of nonsense, and the most extraordinary beast, the most bizarre of fairies, may happily inhabit his never-never land. A child sees a lion, a sheep, and a rabbit in a zoo. Why should a prince named Udo, struck with a spell, not combine them into the same beast, dine on watercress sandwiches, and try to lash his tail? Or the child sees a gull in flight and imagines that Peter Pan can fly like the bird. If Peter should lose his shadow, why should it not be reattached to his ankles? Limited in experience, children must fill the gaps with fantasies, with whimsies. The things they see around them, the animals in the zoo, a shadow, a sewing kit, are the real foundations on which they build their dreams. Both Milne and Barrie, thanks to long memories refreshed by their own children, managed to write of Prince Udo and Peter Pan with a whimsy which was unbounded and yet uncloying.

But Milne and Barrie, akin in whimsy, differ in their moods. Comparing *Once on a Time* to the story *Peter and Wendy* or to the play *Peter Pan* is rather like comparing Wilde's *The Importance of Being Earnest* to Shakespeare's *A Winter's Tale*. Milne is generally playful, occasionally wistful, never sad. Even when Belvane wishes to put a spell on her enemy, Udo, she chooses a gentle spell: " 'I wish,' she said, and there was a terrible smile in her eyes, 'I wish that something very—very *humorous* shall happen to Prince Udo on his journey.'" A terrible smile but not such a terrible wish. Barrie, on the other hand, moves from cheerfulness to wistfulness to outright sadness. Tinker Bell is droll and saucy when she shouts "silly ass" at Wendy; but, when she drinks poison to save Peter's life, she becomes the tragic symbol of fairyland threatened by disbelief and saved at the last possible moment only because some children (not all) believe in fairies and clap their hands.

Along with the sadness in Barrie is menace, terror, evil. The Indians collect the scalps of little boys until Peter rescues Tiger Lily and wins the gratitude of the tribe. Captain Hook, who has lost his arm to Peter, demands a gruesome trophy in exchange— Peter's life and by hook, crook, and a bottle of poison, he nearly gets his wish. Tinker Bell gloats when Wendy, her rival for Peter's affections, is struck by an arrow. Peter pretends that with every breath he can kill a hated grown-up; furious at Wendy when she wants to leave him, he breathes in rapid gulps. After all, says Barrie in his last sentence, "children are gay and innocent and heartless."

The myths and fairy tales which inspired both Milne and Barrie contain sadness and terror as well as joy—"The Ugly Duckling," "Beauty and the Beast," "The Little Mermaid"—tortured animals, bewitched princes, lost children. Milne, in his use of such materials, resembles the anonymous author who rewrote Robert Browning's "The Pied Piper of Hamelin" with a happy ending and restored the children to their parents. Barrie resembles the original author, who left the children imprisoned in the mountain and the parents grieving in childless Hamelin. But Milne's method represents a conscious choice, a self-imposed limitation, rather than a weakness. In *Once on a Time* he has built a cottage instead of a mansion. By limiting his materials, by selecting them with the utmost care, he avoided the risk of choosing worm-eaten timbers or rusty nails, or of building with such a profusion of wood, stones, and bricks, doors, gables, and dormers, that he achieved variety at the expense of charm. He has built modestly, but he has built well. A summer house? A house for many summers—as many, we hope, as the gold doubloons in a pirate's buried chest.

CHAPTER 5

Whisper Who Dares

I When We Were Very Young

THOUGH *Once on a Time* appeared in 1917, it was not until 1924 that Milne completed and published a book expressly for children, *When We Were Very Young*. Only in 1920 had the birth of Christopher Robin provided an inspiration and an audience in his own house. Even then, he did not anticipate writing a book for his son. He began with a single poem, "Vespers," which he casually handed to his wife, who rushed it to *Vanity Fair* and received a check for fifty dollars. It was not long before countless mothers were reading to uncountable children: "Hush! Hush! Whisper who dares! Christopher Robin is saying his prayers."[1]

After a few months, Milne wrote a second poem, "The Dormouse and the Doctor," for Rose Fyleman, a noted children's editor, who urged him to additional efforts—if possible, a book. Reluctantly, Milne obliged her. In his introduction to *When We Were Very Young*, he explains how he had found some of his subjects. It seems that Christopher Robin liked to visit a lake near his house and to feed a certain swan which he named "Pooh" (he had not yet attached the name to his teddy bear). "Well," wrote Milne, "I should have told you that there are six cows who come down to Pooh's lake every afternoon to drink, and of course they say 'Moo' as they come. So I thought to myself one fine day, walking with my friend Christopher Robin, 'Moo rhymes with Pooh! Surely there is a bit of poetry to be got out of that?' "[2] There was more than a bit. Though he dropped his proposed rhyme of "moo" and "Pooh," he wrote a poem to the six cows called "Summer Afternoon" (and celebrated other cows in "The King's Breakfast" and "The Invaders"); a poem called "The Mirror" to the swan; and, in fact, forty-two poems besides "Vespers" and "The Dormouse and the Doctor."

Poems so inspired, we might think, would result in childish jingles, suitable perhaps for reciting to an uncritical son of three but hardly fit for the cold permanence of print. But Milne was always a conscientious craftsman. As he said in his autobiography: "*When We Were Very Young* is not the work of a poet becoming playful, nor of a lover of children expressing his love, nor of a prose-writer knocking together a few jingles for the little ones, it is the work of a light-verse writer taking his job seriously even though he is taking it into the nursery." Milne's American publisher is not exaggerating when he claims that *When We Were Very Young* has "probably been read more widely than any other book of verse for children published in our time." In its first year, from November, 1924, to November, 1925, it ran through fifty-two editions; it has never been out of print; it is still available separately or bound with *Now We Are Six* in *The World of Christopher Robin* or as one of the four volumes sharing a single slip-case in *The Pooh Library*.

Though the book is dedicated to Christopher Robin, only "Sand-Between-the-Toes," "Buckingham Palace," "Hoppity," and "Vespers" address him by name. Other poems, "At Home," "Brownie," "Independence," "Nursery Chairs," and "Halfway Down," appear to be spoken by him. Others concern such real or imaginary children as Percy ("Corner-of-the-Street"), James ("Disobedience"), John ("Happiness"), Emmeline ("Before Tea"), and Mary Jane ("Rice Pudding"); and still others, too numerous to list in full, deal not with children but with butterflies ("Twinkletoes"), animals ("The Four Friends"), flowers ("Daffodowndilly"), fairies ("Water-Lilies"), fairy-tale royalty ("The King's Breakfast"), or toys ("Teddy Bear").

All of the forty-four poems can be roughly divided into two classes—those about the things which a small child does, and those about the things which he pretends—though at times the same poem may slide from truth to fantasy. For example, in "Puppy and I" Christopher has a conversation with a man he meets on one of his walks; he meets a horse and talks to him just as if the animal were a man; then he declines an invitation from rabbits to look for oats but joins a puppy to "roll and play." It is thus in the life of a small child. The hedge which divides reality from make-believe is easily climbed or clipped.

Whether playing in puddles or talking to horses, rabbits, and a puppy, whether walking on the beach with his father or lying in wait for Brownies, the child of these poems—Christopher, John, Jack, Emmeline, or Mary Jane—is persuasive and real. He is not a sentimentalized child, impossibly good or oppressively cute. Only "Vespers," the poem which launched the volume and which later merited its own separate edition, threatens in its first stanza to cloy with an excess of "little's": "Little Boy kneels at the foot of the bed,/Droops on the little hands little gold head."[3] But the too angelic portrait is promptly shattered when Christopher almost forgets to bless his Daddy and starts to peep through his fingers at Nanny's gown on the door.

Avoiding sentimentality, Milne also avoids the opposite extreme of condescension. He never looks down from the Olympian eminence of maturity to treat a child's follies as the amusing antics of a puppy or a kitten. He never intrudes what he calls "that strange but uninteresting person," the author, except in a single poem, "Sand-between-the-Toes"; and here he neither sentimentalizes nor patronizes but simply recounts the time when he and Christopher Robin walked on the beach. As Annie Moore wrote in *Literature Old and New for Children*, his spell is unbroken "by skeptical comment or patronizing assent."[4]

If Milne was the father of the Christopher Robin poems, the mother was not Mrs. Milne, who curiously goes unmentioned, but that venerable and half-legendary lady known as Mother Goose, whom some scholars identify with Queen Goosefoot, the mother of Charlemagne. The influence of "Simple Simon," "Jack and Jill," "Little Jack Horner," and other nursery rhymes is both pervasive and beneficial. To achieve the lilting rhythms which children love and effortlessly memorize, Milne and Mother Goose have resorted to similar devices of versification. In Mother Goose, the lines "Hickory, dickory, dock,/The mouse ran up the clock," compare with some lines from Milne:

> Hoppity, hoppity, hop.
> Whenever I tell him
> Politely to stop it, he
> Says he can't possibly stop.[4]

In both poets the pell-mell lines, the insistent rhymes and alliterations, capture the frantic motion of a mouse or a boy. But Milne is a much more varied and skillful craftsman than Mother

Goose. His ingenious rhyme of "stop it, he" with the two "hop-pity's" of the first line is no less effective for being concealed. What the eye overlooks, the ear records. In other poems, his lines range from one or two brisk and emphatic words as in "Happiness,"

> And that
> (Said John)
> Is
> That,[6]

to a rolling hexameter in the last stanza of "The Island": "There's nobody else in the world, and the world was made for me." His rhymes are inventive and often unconventional. Long before Ogden Nash and after Byron's *Don Juan*, he manufactures such rhymes as "dormouse" and "e-nor-mouse," "foxes" and "sockses." Or, a little like T. H. White when he intrudes an anachronism into a dignified medieval landscape, he may carefully establish a rhyme scheme and then cascade into unrhymed lines and strange typography:

> BUT SOMETIMES
> I wish
> That they wouldn't.[7]

Milne is also indebted to Mother Goose for some of his characters, but he always engages them in new adventures. In his "Little Bo-Peep and Little Boy Blue," the famous shepherdess and shepherd meet to discuss lost sheep and decide to marry instead of tending their flocks. In "Disobedience," a Mother Goose king and queen offer condolences to a twentieth-century boy whose own mother has disobeyed him and gone astray in her motor car:

> King John
> Put up a notice,
> "LOST or STOLEN or STRAYED!
> JAMES JAMES
> MORRISON'S MOTHER
> SEEMS TO HAVE BEEN MISLAID.[8]

In brief, Milne has surpassed Mother Goose as a model, improving her versification, updating her characters, and producing shapely poems instead of infectious jingles.

He also appears to have used some later models. Christina Rossetti writes in an untitled poem from *Sing-Song*:

> In a golden crown,
> And a scant green gown
>   While the spring blows chilly,
> Lady Daffadown,
> Sweet Daffadowndilly.[9]

And Milne in a poem whose very title suggests her influence, "Daffodowndilly," writes:

> She wore her yellow sun-bonnet,
> She wore her greenest gown;
> She turned to the south wind
> And curtsied up and down.[10]

The two poets resemble each other not only in individual poems but in their view of the countryside, its flowers, and its animals. Like many of the best nature poets, they were city dwellers who sometimes visited the country; and they wrote, therefore, not with the jaded familiarity of a farmer or a dairyman, but with a freshness and awe which led them to personify flowers as ladies and to look upon even the commonplace cow with affectionate wonder. Water lilies, primroses, violets, and bluebells spill through the poems of Milne; and he views the cow as "breathing the early morning air/And leaving it still sweeter there." Lilies, sweet peas, goldenrod, snowdrops, and flag-flowers entwine the poems of Christina; and she promises the sweet-breathed cow a garland of cowslips in return for her milk.

But Milne is the better children's poet. As a craftsman, Christina is little superior to Mother Goose. Most of her songs, naïve, unstudied, charm us with their spontaneity; but a few of them read like rough drafts, hummed or jotted between her household duties and never polished. The effect can be ludicrous instead of artless:

> My baby has a mottled fist.
>   By baby has a neck in creases;
> My baby kisses and is kissed,
>   For he's the very thing for kisses.[11]

Had Milne wished to write a poem about a kissable baby, as in "Vespers" he wrote about a kissable three-year-old, he would not have given the child a mottled fist and a creased neck, which suggest a little old man; and his last line would have rippled with grace or wit and climaxed with a strong rhyme, instead of lumbering with the flat colloquialism of "For he's the very thing for kisses."

Milne's flowers and cows recall Christina Rossetti; but his wild animals—bear, lion, elephant, fox, wallaby, mingo, bison—recall Hilaire Belloc and his *Bad Child's Book of Beasts*. But Milne has designed *When We Were Very Young* for children who, on the whole, are well behaved; and his beasts, though various and often carnivorous, are rarely inclined to a diet of human beings. He has, to be sure, a Belloc-style poem called "Lines and Squares," in which a little boy walks down the street and tries not to step on a crack, because of the bears "who wait at the corners all ready to eat/The sillies who tread on the lines of the street." The bears, as described by Milne and drawn by Shepard, are not Winnie-the-Poohs; they are hungry, and not for honey. But the boy avoids the cracks and evades the would-be diners; in Belloc, he would probably have missed his step and become dinner.

The lilt of Mother Goose, the rustic wonders of Christina Rossetti, the varied bestiary of Belloc: Milne has read and borrowed but remained himself, an adaptor and not an imitator. Guiltless of imitating poets, he is guilty, however, of a sometimes obnoxious attempt to imitate babytalk. "Because" becomes "cos" not once but four times in "The Christening." "Important" becomes "portant" in "Lines and Squares"; and, more annoyingly, "nothing" is reduced to "nuffin" in "Market Square." Although children may drop the first syllable of a word, omit a "g," or pronounce a "th" as an "f," an author of forty-two who adopts such mannerisms resembles an overfond parent instead of a poet.

But Milne's occasional lapses hardly diminish the magic of Christopher Robin, the real little boy whose realistic portrait unifies and sweetens *When We Were Very Young* to the stature of a small classic. Many of Shepard's illustrations now seem humorously dated—an automobile of the 1920's, a nurse in a flowing hood, Christopher Robin in his Buster Brown hat. But the child himself, like Little Orphan Annie, does not show age. Today's adolescents have different tastes from those their grandparents had in 1924, but small children still visit zoos, ride tricycles, count cows, and refuse to eat rice pudding; they still daydream about pirates, knights, and talking animals. Admittedly, Christopher Robin seems a trifle quaint to them, a trifle delicate in his dress-like tunic—He *is* a boy, isn't he? they ask their parents—but his quaintness and delicacy do not remove him from their under-standing: like a new neighbor, strange of dress but not unfriendly, he is still a child with whom they can talk and play.

II Now We Are Six

To write a sequel is to risk the Heffalump-pit of imitation: of imitating oneself. But Milne in *Now We Are Six* (1927) avoids the pit. For Christopher Robin has grown from three to six and has made new friends. No longer protected by his father or Nanny, he explores the countryside, himself a protector of girls and teddy bears, or he ventures uncompanioned to newt, fish, or visit Farmer Middleton. More important, he has outgrown his babytalk (and so has the author, except for the Dedication to Anne Darlington, "Because She Is So Speshal," and a few "cos's" ascribed to Pooh).

Among his new friends are a trio of little girls: Ann Darlington, a real little girl of seven who lived next door to the Milnes and who receives not only the Dedication but two poems, "Buttercup Days" and "The Morning Walk"; Elizabeth Ann, who departs on a difficult quest to find the answer to the question, "How did God begin?" and learns the answer from her doll Jennifer; and, finally, the unfortunate Jane, whom people are always asking, "Have you been a *good* girl?"; though, as Jane logically observes, had she been bad, "Should I be likely to say if I had?" There are also friends out of books, kings and knights, physicians and sailors and charcoal burners; and friends from the out of doors, cats, hens, fish, newts, beetles, and especially bears—big bears covered with fur and ready for hibernation, urban bears and rustic, startling bears and startled, bears who are brothers and bears who are unrelated.

And, of course, there is Winnie-the-Pooh, an old friend with a new coat of fur. He appears as the unnamed Teddy Bear of *When We Were Very Young*. He reappears in 1926 as the hero of *Winnie-the-Pooh*, and now he makes his triumphant return to poetry as an ursine alter ego to the growing up Christopher Robin. In addition to sharing "Us Two" and "The Friend" with his master, he graces twenty-four of the Shepard illustrations, some of which illustrate poems like "The Charcoal-Burner" and "The Engineer" in which he is not even mentioned, and two of which make him appear to be the speaker of the poem "Furry Bear," which Milne intended to be spoken by a little boy to an unidentified bear in a zoo.

In view of Pooh's pervasiveness, Milne could justly write: "Pooh wants us to say that he thought it was a different book; and he hopes you won't mind, but he walked through it one day, looking for his friend Piglet, and sat down on some of the pages by mistake."[12] It might be argued that a teddy bear is more appropriate to the three-year-old Christopher Robin of *When We Were Very Young* than to the boy of six, but the answer is that Pooh has ceased to seem a mere stuffed animal. He is more of an individual than Anne Darlington or the misunderstood Jane; and, after his beloved master, he stoutly dominates *Now We Are Six.*

But the charm and freshness of *Now We Are Six,* the fact that it is both a distinguished sequel and a superior book in its own right, are more than a matter of assembling attractive new characters with old characters who have aged becomingly. The story poems of kings and knights and shipwrecked sailors, designed for children of six, and even ten, are considerably more than the slight anecdotes of *When We Were Very Young;* they are fully developed tales, almost ballads, with well-defined unheroic heroes. "King John's Christmas," for example, presents a ruler of much more complexity than the king who advertised a reward for James Morrison Weatherby George Duprez's lost mother. For the "very young," a king must be painted in black and white; for a child of six, grays are possible and often preferable. King John is neither all virtuous nor all wicked; "he was not a good man" and "he had his little ways," yet he is pathetic when he writes a request to Father Christmas and signs it "not 'Johannes R.' but very humbly, 'JACK,'" and decidedly sympathetic when he gets his heart's desire,

A BIG, RED,
INDIA-RUBBER
BALL.[13]

In addition, the story poems no longer necessarily contain children for their heroes. In other words, they reflect the fact that, as children mature and leave the nursery, they learn to project themselves into persons foreign to their actual experience. They can read about pirates and Indians, sailors and soldiers, without the intermediary of a Peter Pan. The story poems in *When We Were Very Young* generally included children. "Disobedience" introduced a king, a queen, and a prince; but its hero was a little boy. "The King's Breakfast" contained no children, it is true, but its heroine was a friendly and obliging cow which, to a small child, is the next thing to another child and far more companionable than most adults. The story poems of the second volume, however, abound with adults. There are neither children nor cows in "King John's Christmas" or in "The Knight Whose Armour Didn't Squeak." "The Old Sailor" is wrecked on an island without youthful company. The only children in "King Hilary and the Beggarman" appear in the expectation of Hilary when he hears a knock at the gate and wonders if his little subjects can be bringing him cobnuts. No. It is a beggarman with one red stocking.

Furthermore, in *Now We Are Six* Milne seems less indebted to Mother Goose than to the more complicated craft of Robert Louis Stevenson's *A Child's Garden of Verses*. Always a careful craftsman, Milne rivals Stevenson in the glossiness of his lines, the assurance and yet the surprise of his rhymes, the variety of his forms. In "King John's Christmas," he uses an elaborate ten-line stanza which rhymes *abcbdefffe* and resourcefully pairs such words as "near and far" and "particular." In "The Good Little Girl" he varies his rhyme scheme from stanza to stanza and dares, from time to time, to replace his rhymes with a thumping refrain, "Have you been a *good* girl?"

Equal to Stevenson in craftsmanship, Milne surpasses him in characterization; in the ease with which he enters his subjects, whether children or adults, laughs with their laughter, stomps his foot with their pique; and avoids the preaching which makes a poem seem a lesson. He entitles a poem "The Good Little Girl" with intentional irony, since the little girl emphatically does not welcome the question of her elders: "Have you been a *good* girl?" His rare morals are humorous and not sententious as, for example, in "Twice Times," a poem about a Good Bear who learns his Twice Times One and a Bad Bear who leaves his buttons undone, until finally the bears change places, Good becoming Bad, and Bad, Good:

There may be a Moral, though some say not;
I think there's a moral, though I don't know what.
But if one gets better, as the other gets wuss,
These Two Little Bears are just like Us.
For Christopher remembers up to Twice Times Ten . . . .
But I keep forgetting where I've put my pen.[14]

Stevenson, on the other hand, too often allows the voice of the righteous parent to speak through the child and produces a little prig who mouths platitudes of virtue and good sense. His parental intrusions perhaps explain the fact that most children like *all* of *Now We Are Six* and *part* of *A Child's Garden of Verses*. Such deadly serious titles as "Whole Duty of Children," "A Good Boy," and "Good and Bad Children" suggest to a child that poetry is one more method to teach and chastise him. When he comes to a line like, "I never said an ugly word, but smiled and stuck to play," he is hardly to be blamed if he flings down the book with his first ugly word.

To summarize Milne's achievement as a poet for children: *When We Were Very Young* and *Now We Are Six* have captured a bright, appealing child in his everyday moments as no other poet could have captured him. *In his everyday moments* is also a clue to Milne's limitations, for he has not attempted the heights and the depths of a child's experience, such as sadness. In the Christopher Robin poems, there is pique, disappointment, and occasional loneliness, but there is no real sadness. For example, we may compare Milne's "Forgotten" with Eugene Field's "Little Boy Blue." Both poems concern the toys in a nursery which await the return of a master. In Milne:

Big Kings and Little Kings,
Brown Bears and Black,
All of them waiting
Till John comes back.[15]

In Field:

The little toy dog is covered with dust,
But sturdy and stanch he stands;
And the little toy soldier is red with rust,
And the musket moulds in his hands.[16]

John, who has been skipping rope and playing ball, returns at night and contentedly goes to bed with his toys. Little Boy Blue, on the other hand, has died; and his toys must wait and wait for the master who never returns. The happy ending in Milne epitomizes him as a writer for children. We have seen the identical method in *Once on a Time*, where even the wicked Belvane is forgiven by the princess and allowed to marry the king. Milne himself had enjoyed a tranquil childhood and a loving bond with his father, and he liked to think of his son as repeating his own experience. Whatever despairs may have troubled the real Christopher Robin and escaped his father's eye, the boy in the poems is often gay, sometimes grave, but never sorrowful.

If Milne has omitted the depths of a child's sadness, he has also omitted the heights of his wonder; he has missed his closeness to the mysteries of creation, to what Wordsworth called the "clouds of glory." Milne cannot approach the magic of Walter de la Mare, whose language—hushed, hesitant, plaintive—tinkles like elfin pipes or water turning enchanted millwheels, and whose Listeners inhabit a ruinous castle instead of a brightly lit nursery. Christopher Robin looks for a Brownie, but he limits his search to the safety of his own bedroom. Milne and De la Mare wrote in the same decades and died in the same year (1956), both of them fabulists in an era of realism. But the poems of Milne are more humorous than fabulous.

Moreover, his very humor is fettered to earth, like a bunch of colored balloons attached to strings and kept from the bouncing winds. He lacks the inspired nonsense of Edward Lear's Jumblies, who went to sea in a sieve, and Lewis Carroll's Jabberwocky, which burbled through the woods. Lear and Carroll were latter-day and highly original mythologists who invented outlandish monsters for their seas and forests. Milne, on the other hand, prefers the brownies and fairies of traditional folklore; moreover, he prefers to treat them in their tamer, tidier aspects. In the books about Pooh, to be sure, a colored balloon sometimes makes its escape, both literally (carrying Pooh) and figuratively (carrying humor to heights of nonsense); but the infamous Heffalump is only a mispronounced elephant and the Woozle is hunted but never seen.

Milne's limitations, however, are those of genius. Within his chosen range he is unsurpassed. Christina Rossetti, Stevenson, De la Mare, Lear, and Carroll: masters all of them—but which one has created the equal of Christopher Robin, who belongs to the world's children as Pooh belongs to Christopher? The international writer Jan de Hartog, in his novel *The Distant Shore*, tells how the captain of a Dutch tug in World War II—an imaginary captain but one who reflected his own experiences—hushed his fears and found the courage to face a German submarine by reciting those incantatory lines: "Hush! Hush! Whisper who dares!/Christopher Robin is saying his prayers." As Mary Hill Arbuthnot wrote: "Many poets achieve greater lyric beauty, more delicate imagery, and deeper feeling for the child's inner world. The child should know such poets as well as A. A. Milne. But certainly we shall never encounter a writer who understands more completely the curious composite of gravity and gaiety, of supreme egotism and occasional whimsy that is the young child."[17]

CHAPTER 6

The Peerless Pooh

THE AMERICAN INDIANS of Colonial days believed that bear cubs were born as shapeless masses of flesh and fur which their mothers must knead, lick, and caress into the shape of bears. Similarly, Winnie-the-Pooh did not spring plump and perfect from his author's brain; he grew by degrees and climaxed a carefully mastered craft after Milne's apprenticeship period. Milne's first book of sketches, *Lovers in London*, was a debacle, but he learned from his failure and became the polished essayist of *By Way of Introduction*. His first play, *Wurzel-Flummery*, was a simple-minded farce, but he climbed to that brilliant comedy, *Mr. Pim Passes By*. Even the Christopher Robin poems owe much of their skill to the apprenticeship he served as a sometime light versifier for *Punch*.

Most admirers of Pooh are not aware that 1925 saw the publication of a volume called *A Gallery of Children*, a bloodless and Pooh-less book of stories which taught the author to write the better stories about his famous bear. Mildly enjoyed in the 1920's and reprinted in the 1930's as two separate volumes, *The Princess and the Apple Tree* and *The Magic Hill*, *A Gallery* is now forgotten and unlamented, consigned to oblivion by those final arbiters of juvenile literature, children; and for good reason. Except for Poor Anne, whose hair turns an unbecoming red, the little heroes and heroines are as charming but unlikely as Hummel figures, whose place is a china shelf and not in a book of stories. They strike a becoming pose in their miniature gallery, and then, unlike the Gingham Dog and the Calico Cat, they cease to move, for the author refuses to prod them after Heffalumps or threaten them with bears on street corners. Even such a fairy tale as "The Princess and the Apple-Tree" is less a tale than a sketch. It holds enchantments, yes: the Princess' lowborn lover is turned by her father, the king, into an apple tree. But the ease with

86

which she changes him to his old shape eliminates any suspense: she simply cries "Comfort me!", embraces the trunk, and, lo, he becomes a man and a bridegroom in two paragraphs. "A Voyage to India" perfectly illustrates the inertia and the consequent failure of *A Gallery*. Jane Ann, living with her Aunt Mary in England, plans to visit her parents in India. She says good-by to her Rabbit, packs her provisions for the journey (a box of chocolates), and prepares to depart for the land of the tiger. She never departs:

> Looking out of the window next morning, Rabbit saw that it was raining.
> "Perhaps she won't go now," he said, and he was very excited.
> After breakfast Jane Ann looked out of the window, too.
> "It will stop soon," she said cheerfully.
> And she stood there waiting for it to stop. . . .[1]

A child accustomed to the aerial flights of Walt Disney's cinematic Mary Poppins and the submarine exploits of Ivan Tors's Flipper will not be content with Mary Jane in the house; he will want her to go to India, even if she catches a cold.

But Milne at least learned from his first book of stories for children that his next must assemble characters who were lively instead of pretty, and that he must characterize them by incidents as well as descriptions and dialogue. But where could he find such characters? For his hero, he looked in Christopher Robin's nursery. Since the age of one, the child had owned a teddy bear, round of tummy, vacant of eye, and by this time considerably battered by thumpings up and down the stairs. The bear, as yet unnamed, had made a telling appearance in *When We Were Very Young*. Shepard's illustration had shown him standing in front of a mirror to lament his adiposity and wrapped in a short cloak with a single button which appears to have been buttoned with difficulty, and Milne had written:

> A bear, however hard he tries,
> Grows tubby without exercise.
> Our Teddy Bear is short and fat
> Which is not to be wondered at;
> He gets what exercise he can
> By falling off the ottoman,
> But generally seems to lack
> The energy to clamber. . . .[2]

Together Milne and Shepard had launched a benevolent monster —to the world, a benevolent clown—who would jealously track them to the end of their careers: Winnie-the-Pooh, the nonpareil of bears.

Bears in literature, of course, are as old as recorded history. In early times they were actually worshiped by many primitive societies. The ancient Finns looked upon them as demigods of the forest, not unlike the Greek satyrs and the Roman fauns, while even today, in the northern islands of Japan, the primitive Anou alternate between venerating and hunting them for their skins. From worship to myth is an easy and logical step: that which is worshiped becomes commemorated in stories and songs. Greek mythologists, perhaps reflecting a prehistoric animal cult, held that the god Zeus, who loved the nymph Callisto, transformed her into a bear to protect her from Hera's wrath; and then, to keep her son Arcas, a hunter, from killing her by mistake, they also changed the boy and placed both mother and son in the sky as the constellations Great Bear and Little Bear.

The distance from myth to fairy tale, from stories told for superstitious adults to stories told for gullible children, is long and hard to traverse, and many a mythological beast has lost his way in the intervening morasses; but the durable bear has successfully made the journey to reappear in nursery tales like that of Goldilocks, a little girl who enters an empty house, gorges herself on porridge, and falls asleep in a middle-sized bed, only to be awakened, scolded, forgiven, and welcomed by the returning owners, Mama Bear, Papa Bear, and Baby Bear. In most of his appearances—worship, myth, and fairy tale—the bear is benignant, clever, favorable to man when properly propitiated, and, even when slain, valued for his hide.

Throughout the centuries the bear has enjoyed an exceptionally good press, while the unfortunate wolf has been shown devouring grandmothers or blowing down the houses of defenseless pigs. For example, in J. R. R. Tolkein's *The Hobbit*, which accurately reflects English folklore, a helpful were-bear protects the Hobbit on his quest for the dragon's trove; but wolves are allied with the spiders and gnomes which block his path and try to destroy him. Perhaps the bear has been preferred to the wolf because, when small, he is an irresistible elf of whirling fur and, when large, he manages to make clumsiness seem clowning. In contrast to the pack-running wolf, he is a doughty loner, an individualist who commands respect.

Milne's bear, to be sure, is no grizzly from the back woods, nor even a fairy-tale beast, but a teddy bear. Children have always played with toy animals, carved from wood or ivory or woven of cloth and stuffed with feathers, though it was only when the nickname of that great sportsman, Theodore Roosevelt, was attached to toy bears that they came to be called Teddy and surpassed all other animals in popularity with the young. Children love them because they are warm and furry and also because they are docile and manageable. (It has even been argued by sociologists that the singing Beatles are teddy bear symbols—fuzzy, cuddlesome, safe.) Teddy bears neither bite nor have to be bathed, trimmed, and sprayed for fleas; they never disagree and thus they provide the ideal listener and the boon companion. Christopher Robin, in story as well as in fact, could bump Pooh up the stairs without any risk of teeth clamped in his leg. Most of a child's life is taking orders; in the playroom, he prefers to give them. By their very nature, teddy bears are gentle; and Pooh is the gentlest of his tribe. He is little akin to the powerful creatures of worship and myth, or even the goodhearted but petulant Mama and Papa of the Goldilocks story. As a teddy bear, he represents the ultimate taming of a wild animal into a children's toy. But, shorn of his claws, he becomes a great clown.

I   Winnie-the-Pooh

"What about a story?" said Christopher Robin.

"*What* about a story?" I said.

"Could you very sweetly tell Winnie-the-Pooh one?"

"I suppose I could," I said. "What sort of stories does he like?"

"About himself. Because he's *that* sort of Bear."[3]

It was not hard for Milne, who had profited from his mistakes in *A Gallery of Children,* to tell a whole book of stories about Pooh. *That* sort of animal had appealed to him since his own childhood when his brother Ken was given *Reynard the Fox.* "We both read it. When, forty years later, I wrote a book called *Winnie--the-Pooh,* and saw Shephard's drawing of Pooh, the bear, standing on the branch of a tree outside Owl's house, I remembered all that *Reynard the Fox* and *Uncle Remus* and the animal stories in *Aunt Judy's Magazine* had meant to us."[4]

Then, too, the actual teddy bear in Christopher Robin's nursery now had several names, and such a bear deserved several stories. Christopher had stolen the name "Pooh" from his pet swan and attached it to his toy, whom the name suited admirably because, as Milne observed, it resembled the sniff of a bear when he wishes to dislodge a fly from his sensitive nose. The "Winnie" was borrowed from another animal, a bear in the London Zoo. Thus provided with a pair of names and with hyphens to join them, Winnie-the-Pooh was further designated "Edward" because he was a teddy bear and in England "Teddy" is the nickname for Edward. Finally, he was sometimes called "Sanders," because he lived under that name in the forest—that is, "he had the name over the door in gold letters, and lived under it."

When Pooh appeared in his own book, not only did he enjoy a multiplicity of names, but he reveled in illustrations by Ernest Shepard which have become inseparable from him and his friends and which have reappeared in all subsequent editions. Before Shepard made his sketches, he visited the animals in Christopher Robin's nursery and found his prototypes for Piglet, Tigger, Kanga, Roo, and Eeyore as well as Pooh (though not for Owl and Rabbit). Being an artist and not a photographer, he skillfully altered—and thereby improved—his models. He reduced Piglet's head and elongated his snout. He broadened Eeyore's rear and Kanga's pouch. Most important, he plumpened Pooh's stomach, shortened his arms, and lent to his button-eyes the vacancy of an inveterate and none-too-intelligent dreamer or, when a honey jar is in sight, the amiable calculation of a none-too-intelligent schemer. Shepard's animals are simple drawings in black and white, but their simplicity is that of Milne's writing, the simplicity of genius, of capturing essentials in a few unerring strokes, in the way of Thurber with his woeful hounds and puzzled hippopotamuses. Ironically, Milne was not always an admirer of Shepard. During his days with *Punch*, he remarked to the art editor: "What on earth do you see in this man? He's perfectly hopeless." "You wait," said the editor; and the day arrived when Shepard was Milne's own choice to illustrate his books.[5]

It goes without saying that Pooh, in text as well as illustrations, remains triumphantly and uproariously the hero of his book, a Sancho Panza without a Don Quixote, but one who has found his own windmills to tilt. Hinting for honey, breasting a flood atop a

jar, or searching for Eeyore's tail, he is all the funnier because he
is not aware of his fun:

> "Owl," said Pooh solemnly of the lost tail, "you made a mistake.
> Somebody did want it."
> "Who,"
> "Eeyore. My dear friend Eeyore. He was—he was fond of it."
> "Fond of it?"
> "Attached to it," said Winnie-the-Pooh sadly.[6]

But a clown, even an accidental one like Pooh, requires an audience to evoke his buffooneries; to inspire, reflect, and amplify; to
act as foils. Pooh has a host of friends who are jesters in their own
right and foils to the jests of the master: Owl, the sage of the tree-
tops, whose old world residence has "both a knocker *and* a bell-
pull"; Piglet, an unabashed coward who reluctantly joins Pooh in
schemes to track a Woozle or trap a Heffalump; Rabbit, whose
friends and relations include beetles, mice, hedgehogs, squirrels,
and frogs; the motherly Kanga, whom a modern psychologist might
accuse of overprotecting her baby Roo; the irrepressible Tigger,
whose bounce is as friendly and breathtaking as that of a Great
Dane; and the misanthropic Eeyore, who can never say good
morning without the reservation, "If it *is* a good morning."

Pooh and his friends constitute what Ben Jonson would have
called "humour" characters. In each of them, one characteristic is
exaggerated for humorous effect—Pooh's gluttony, Owl's pedantry,
Piglet's timidity, Tigger's energy. A story for children allows small
space for detailed characterization; indeed, children lack the
patience for inner monologues or page-long descriptions. The
wonder is that Milne, working within such rigid limitations and
forced to characterize with broad, brief strokes, has managed to
create individuals instead of types. His secret is that he constantly
reveals character through action. The animals meet, talk, and characterize themselves with tricks of speech—Pooh is diffident and
halting except on the subject of food; Owl, verbose and pedantic—
but they plan or adventure even while they talk. As in most books
loved by children, action is never made to wait on words. The
action may not be large. Pooh and Piglet may spend a chapter
walking in circles. But always something is in doubt, something
threatens or promises. For example in "Expotition to the North
Pole," the characters talk at length about boots, gorse-bushes, and

thistles; but all the while they advance the story: they plan, conduct, and conclude an "expotition" to find a pole, even if not the North Pole. In addition to the animal characters, there is Christopher Robin, who comes up a hill or down from a tree when his friends get in trouble and, like a deus ex machina, extricates and advises them. Human beings as a rule should not be mingled with talking animals, as Kenneth Grahame discovered when he locked Mr. Toad in a castle with human jailers and succeeded, momentarily, in making Toad appear implausible and the jailers impossible. Christopher Robin could not be denied admittance to a story about his own animals and told for his own benefit. He could, however, be denied importance. Milne, an author as well as a father, has strictly limited his son's appearances and made him unobtrusive and unpatronizing when he does appear; Christopher Robin is a master, yes, but more an observer. "Silly old bear," he calls to Pooh; but he gives a party to honor him with a Special Pencil Case, "pencils in it marked 'B' for Bear, and pencils marked 'HB' for Helping Bear, and pencils marked 'BB' for Brave Bear." It it Pooh's present and Pooh's book.

Such characters—indispensable animals and incidental boy—deserve a setting which befits their antics; and Milne provides for them a forest which is never named but tantalizingly drawn by Shepard, with Piglet's tree house, the pit for Heffalumps, the copse "Where the Woozle Wasn't," and other arresting landmarks noted in bold letters. Enchanted forests are older than literature. In prehistoric and early historic times, forests were actually thought to be enchanted. They were unexplored and, therefore, unexplainable. Out of necessity, man lived close to them or in them and thrived or suffered, it seemed, according to their moods; man chopped their limbs for houses and hollowed their logs for boats but suffered the threat of their beasts, floods, fires, and lightless labyrinths. In the face of such very real and evident dangers, it was only natural to endow them also with unreal dangers. There were wolves—and gods like Faunus who took the shape of wolves. There were turbulent streams—and trolls who lived in the streams and drowned unwary travelers. When the forests were stripped of their terrors by the axes of builders and the sharper tools of reason, the dispossessed monsters took refuge in fairy tales and frightened children now that they could no longer frighten adults.

But, if the enchanted forest still holds memories of man's archetypal fears, it also holds his yearnings, his lost Edens and his unforgotten gods. Cold-eyed reason has robbed the oak of its Dryad, the hill of its Oread—except in the fastness of a fairy tale. Though the gods are reduced to fairies, though Zeus is Oberon and Hermes is Robin Goodfellow, they are not without their gifts and their graces, their little twinklings of the old divine beauty. It is the benignity of the forest and not the threat which Shakespeare has caught in *A Midsummer Night's Dream* and in *As You Like It;* his conjurations result in hilarity and not tragedy, and his banks are "over-canopied with luscious woodbine" and incandescent with wings. The same benignity appeals to Milne:

One day when the sun had come back over the Forest, bringing with it the scent of May, and all the streams of the Forest were tinkling happily to find themselves their own pretty shape again, and the little pools lay dreaming of the life they had seen and the big things they had done, and in the warmth and quiet of the Forest the cuckoo was trying over his voice carefully and listening to see if he liked it, and wood-pigeons were complaining gently to themselves in their lazy comfortable way that it was the other fellow's fault, but it didn't matter very much; on such a day as this Christopher Robin whistled in a special way he had, and Owl came flying out of the Hundred Acre Wood to see what was wanted.[7]

Sensible Christopher Robin knows that the Heffalump and the Woozle exist only in the imagination of Pooh and Piglet. There may be threatening floods, but there are always honey jars to serve as boats. Oak trees spread their branches not to conceal Wizzles but to provide houses for Owl and Piglet. Caves hold Poohs instead of grizzly bears. The forest of Milne is not the haunt of Pan, lying in wait to terrorize travelers, but of animals kinder than the kindest men and of a little boy whose whistle is an incantation.

I   The House at Pooh Corner

Winnie-the-Pooh demanded a sequel. The real-life Christopher Robin clamored for more stories about his adipose bear, and children by the million, American as well as British, agreed that it was time for Christopher's storybook self to march down the stairs with Pooh thumping behind him. Furthermore, that fickle abstraction, sometimes known as the Muse, chose 1928 in which to assume the guise of a fairy godmother and whisper to Milne of never-never lands instead of drawing rooms. In this year he wrote (though not published) *The Ivory Door* and also he returned for the last time to Winnie-the-Pooh and his friends.

The House at Pooh Corner revisits the familiar and beloved characters but engages them in agreeably new adventures—building the house for Eeyore mentioned in the title; searching for Rabbit's friend, Small; inventing a game called Pooh Sticks—and introduces them to a new playmate, Tigger, who occupies a chapter learning what tigers like to eat (extract of malt) and then another chapter trapped in a tree because his tail prevents a graceful descent. Considered together, the Winnie-the-Pooh books, even more than the Christopher Robin poems, represent the summit of Milne's achievement in all fields, a mountain so easily climbed that it seems a hill until we get to the top and find ourselves almost in the clouds. Lewis Carroll had caught the sensible nonsense of childhood; Barrie, the wonder and the wounding sadness. Kenneth Grahame had detailed the forests and fields, the rivers and islands of the English countryside with the accuracy of a naturalist and the language of a poet. But Milne captured, incomparably and enduringly, the frolic and indolence, the sweetness and foolishness, of animals which are also people.

His animals are laughable and, at the same time, lovable. They are laughable because they miniaturize our human eccentricities. Who has not met an over-indulgent Pooh among his acquaintances? Or a fearful Piglet? Or a pessimistic nay-sayer like Eeyore? "I might have known," said Eeyore. "After all, one can't complain. I have my friends. Somebody spoke to me only yesterday. And was it last week or the week before that Rabbit bumped into me and said 'Bother!' The Social Round. Always something going on." Kanga and Owl are miniature adults; Roo and Tigger are miniature children; but Pooh, Piglet, and Eeyore are a curious and beguiling mixture of child and adult, almost as if it were Christopher Robin who had conceived them instead of his father, giving them the independent lives of his father's friends—their own homes, their own livelihoods—but a child's illiteracy ("Heffalump" for "elephant"), fears (Woozles), fondnesses (honey). Thus, the creatures are doubly delightful to children, who find the qualities which annoy them in their parents reduced to unannoying dimensions, and also the weaknesses which they see and forgive in themselves.

A child who resents his mother's overprotectiveness can laugh at
Kanga and sympathize with Roo; a child with a weakness for candy
can understand a bear's fondness for honey and laugh at his strata-
gems to replenish his supply.

But Milne, who loves his animals, never makes them figures of
ridicule: foolish at times, yes; ridiculous, no. They are jesters but
not caricatures. They are not vehicles for mordant satire or farcical
burlesque. Even less than in *Once on a Time* is he writing an
Animal Farm or a *Gulliver's Travels*. His fatherly warmth perme-
ates the book, and his fondness for animals which, furry, hoofed,
pawed, or striped, demand to be hugged instead of scolded. His
animals are lovable because they are loving. Their claws do not
rend, their hooves do not bruise. When Pooh invites Piglet to share
his house, Piglet squeezes his paw. " 'Thank you, Pooh,' he said,
'I should love to.' " They form a startling contrast to the humanized
but diabolical animals of Milne's contemporary, Saki, whose talking cat, Tobermory, collects the scandal about his master's guests
and contemplates blackmail, and whose heroine Laura, reincarnated as an otter, exacts a devilish revenge on a man who has
wronged her. But the animals in Milne are fond of each other and
fonder of Christopher Robin. When Christopher goes to school,
Rabbit and Owl misinterpret his note, "Gon out/backson/bisy/
backson," as a plea for help from a Spotted or Herbaceous Backson
and organize a frantic search to rescue him.

But perhaps the kindliest scene in the book, the scene in which
Milne is speaking his own philosophy through his characters, is
the one in which Tigger has accidentally bounced Eeyore into the
river. After the accident, Pooh, Piglet, and Christopher Robin discuss the incident:

> "Tigger is all right *really*," said Piglet lazily.
> "Of course he is," said Christopher Robin.
> "Everybody is *really*," said Pooh. That's what I think," said Pooh.
> "But I don't suppose I'm right," he said.
> "Of course you are," said Christopher Robin.[8]

In the world at large, Pooh would have been mistaken; obviously,
everybody is not all right. In Milne's forest, and in Milne's own
view at the time, he has spoken the simple truth.

A story without a villain, except for an imagined Heffalump, runs
the risk of resembling a fruitcake that is all sweets and no spices.

But Milne, the gentle ironist, supplies a dousing of rum. Good-natured Pooh is more than merely quaint: he is fat, dumb, and self-indulgent; and every fault which mars his character paradoxically improves him as a character in a book. He is a three-dimensional clown and not a prettified shadow like Walt Disney's interpretation of Bambi. Even Pooh's songs are instinct with jolly egotism:

> I could spend a happy morning
>   Seeing Roo,
> I could spend a happy morning
>   Being Pooh.
> For it doesn't seem to matter,
> If I don't get any fatter
> (And I *don't* get any fatter),
>   What I do.[9]

For Milne to have written four delightful books about his son and Pooh was a literary miracle. To have written a fifth and a sixth might well have thinned and dissipated delight through just such repetition as marred the endless Oz books, which became so stereotyped after the death of the original author, Frank Baum, that his successor, Dorothy Plumly Thompson, came to resemble a duplicating machine. Besides, Christopher Robin was growing up—he was almost eight when *The House at Pooh Corner* appeared; and his days for listening to stories about a little boy and his teddy bear, much less for inspiring such stories, were clearly numbered. Already he had started to fret when schoolmates identified him as the boy with the bear, and indeed he was soon to feel himself a latter-day Little Lord Fauntleroy who, regardless of age, was expected to fit the quaint and childish image in a book. Even his father admitted that the name "Christopher Robin" had come to belong to the public; in the bosom of the family, his son was "Billy Moon." It was time, Milne saw, to say good-by to Pooh and his friends. The final chapter of *The House at Pooh Corner* is Milne's farewell, and the only chapter which mingles sadness with gaiety.

The first paragraph begins, "Christopher Robin was going away. Nobody knew why he was going; nobody knew where he was going. . . ." He has already started to school; now, he is starting on a longer journey: toward manhood. Pooh and Christopher climb to the top of a hill called Galleon's Lap, "the only place in the

Forest where you could sit down carelessly, without getting up again almost at once and looking for somewhere else." Christopher tells a none too attentive Pooh about all the things he has learned and is going to learn in the great world:

> Then, suddenly again, Christopher Robin, who was still looking at the world, with his chin in his hands, called out "Pooh!"
> "Yes?" said Pooh.
> "When I'm—when———Pooh!"
> "Yes, Christopher Robin?"
> "I'm not going to do Nothing any more."
> "Never again?"
> "Well, no so much. They don't let you."[10]

"They don't let you"—parents, teachers, adults in general. The only way to beat them is to join them. So Christopher Robin has to grow up; and Milne, who will keep on writing almost until his death, will never again write books about a little boy and his bear. But we have the author's promise: "But of course, it isn't really Good-bye, because the Forest will always be there . . . and anybody who is Friendly with Bears can find it."

CHAPTER 7

From Mr. Pim to Chloe Marr

EVEN the most ardent fans of Pooh and Christopher Robin are often surprised to learn that the author enjoyed a briefly successful but protracted career as a novelist for adults. Milne's misfortune was that he wrote his two best novels, *Mr. Pim Passes By* (adapted from the play) and *The Red House Mystery*, in the early 1920's and then overshadowed them with his own juveniles:

> If a writer, why not write
> On whatever comes in sight?
> So—the Children's Books: a short
> Intermezzo of a sort:
> When I wrote them, little thinking
> All my years of pen-and-inking
> Would be almost lost among
> Those four trifles for the young.[1]

When he returned to the writing of novels in the 1930's and the 1940's, most of his readers either ignored him or reminded him that what they preferred was another Pooh and not a Mr. Pim. If they did read *Two People, Four Days' Wonder,* and *Chloe Marr,* they justly concluded that he should have said good-by to his novels instead of his juveniles.

Milne succeeds best as a novelist when he limits his canvas to a few people, a short time and a small scene—in other words, when he practices the Aristotelian unities which he learned as a dramatist. Since the time of Shakespeare, both dramatists and novelists have, on occasion, flouted these unities to good effect, skipped a decade between acts, or skimmed to a new country with each new chapter —but not Milne. True, he can fail even when he limits his time and his scene as in *Four Days' Wonder.* More often, however, as in *Mr. Pim Passes By* and *The Red House Mystery,* he seems to draw

power and confidence from his self-imposed restrictions. Like a
Japanese miniaturist who paints a glade instead of a vista, but
compensates for smallness by capturing every flicker of light, every
turn of a leaf, Milne applies his strokes with the certainty of one
who understands his subject in all of its rich minutiae.

Yet his very craftsmanship has worked to discredit him. In the
first decades of the twentieth century, the well-made novel and
the well-made poem fell into disrepute. Plot, it was widely argued,
was an artificial order imposed upon the disorders which constitute
life; and the honest novelist, the realistic novelist, as opposed to
the mere practitioner for the popular magazines, should allow the
thoughts of his characters to assume a chaotic stream of conscious-
ness analogous to a patient's ramblings on a psychoanalyst's couch.
The same considerations, the critics insisted, should bind the poet
to rhymeless and often unpunctuated free verse instead of sonnets
and ballads; to verse which began with an understatement, moved
through a series of ambiguities without visible transitions, and
ended not with a bang but a whimper. Instead of Edith Wharton
and *The Age of Innocence,* this period preferred James Joyce and
Finnegans Wake; instead of the idylls of Tennyson or the monologues of Browning, *The Waste Land* of T. S. Elliot.

The theory that art should reproduce the chaos of life is still
exemplified by the anti-novelists of France, the dramatists of the
absurd, and the Beatnik poets of San Francisco. In such a climate,
it is not likely that Milne's novels—even his good ones—will return
to favor. *The Red House Mystery* is allowed a modest survival in
an inexpensive edition because it is a detective story, and the conventions of the genre still permit a trimly constructed plot and an
unambiguous conclusion. But *Mr. Pim Passes·By,* which in the
space of a single day raises a number of questions about marriage
and morality and answers all of them with satisfying finality, has
not remained in print. Both of the books deserve renewed attention.
In both of them Milne has more than fulfilled his theory of drama
and fiction: he has shaped his materials, arranged, compressed, and
neatened, and made his "characters behave unnaturally, in order
that to the audience, looking in the mirror, they shall seem natural."[2] On the other hand, when he apes the modern convention of
formlessness in *Two People* and *Chloe Marr*—meanders instead of
pursuing a recognizable plot, and ends with a whimper and not a
bang—he fails as a novelist.

I   Mr. Pim Passes By

Mr. Pim Passes By, published in 1921, reverses the usual procedure among writers: it is not a novel from which a play was
adapted, but an adaptation from the play of 1919. Milne has preserved the virtues of his play and strengthened them with the art
of a novelist. In most modern plays, as we have seen, a character
must reveal himself through words and deeds; he is no longer
allowed the soliloquies with which Hamlet verbalized his torments
of conscience and Othello his pangs of jealousy. In a novel, however, the omniscient author may probe, dissect, and explain as he
chooses: in short, reveal the motive behind the word or the deed.

In the play, Mr. Pim appears in the first scene without preamble,
and all we are told of him—and this only in the stage directions—is
that he is "wistful, kindly, gentle, little Mr. Pim, living in some
world of his own whither we cannot follow." But, in the novel, we
do indeed follow him into a world of his own, as he hums to himself and remembers "the wonderful things one seems to have done
and the wonderful things one hopes to do"; and we see him also
in the thoughts of two village boys who watch him pass on his way
to Marden House and almost decide "to tell him to get his hair cut."
Thus, the stage is set in the novel far more effectively than in the
play, and the story which follows is one in which hilariously fallible
or infallible characters enact a beguiling plot.

Mr. Pim calls at Marden House to ask for a letter of introduction.
He has never met the Mardens; he has no connection with them
except that they share a mutual friend. The situation which he finds
in the house and never quite understands concerns Olivia Marden,
whose first husband, Telworthy, was an embezzler and a convict
who presumably drank himself to death in Australia. Olivia is now
happily married to George Marden, a country gentleman whose
ideas are as antiquated as his house. George's niece and ward,
Dinah, wishes to marry a struggling young artist, Brian Strange,
and has brought him down from London to meet her aunt and
uncle. But old-fashioned George likes no art more recent than Sir
Joshua Reynolds, and Brian's Futurism—square clouds and blue
sheep—and his poverty—he has sold one painting—infuriate him.
No niece of *his* shall marry an impoverished Futurist, he concludes.
Olivia, on the other hand, appreciates the young man's modernism
—in fact she is hoping to modernize Marden House with black and

orange curtains—and thinks him more than acceptable as a husband for Dinah.

But Mr. Pim brings distressing news. It seems he has just arrived from Australia with a rascal of a fellow, in trouble with the law, an alcoholic and all that. The man sounds disconcertingly familiar to Olivia. What was his name?

> "Quick, Mr. Pim, quick!"
> A quiet satisfaction spread itself over Mr. Pim's face. What a memory he had for his age! He never forgot a name—never!
> "I've got it" he said, beaming at them. "Telworthy."[3]

And so, Olivia learns that she has two husbands. The complications which follow, the revelation that Olivia is not, after all, a bigamist—Mr. Pim, it seems, has confused "Telworthy" with "Polwittle"—and the manner in which she makes the most of his mistake to prod her husband into accepting Brian are pursued with a zest and zaniness which never descend to farce. At the end of the day, Dinah has Brian, and Olivia has not only her new curtains but a husband shaken into a new awareness of her desirability.

Like most of the best comic novels, *Mr. Pim Passes By* has a theme, a point, a significance. It harnesses laughter to the cart of wisdom. Fielding's *Tom Jones* tickles the funny bone but also examines the mores of eighteenth-century England and ends by suggesting that true morality lies in a kind heart and not in polished manners. Milne, like Fielding, is serious beneath his smiles. George is an amiable relic from the Victorian days when the husband was lord of the manor and the wife existed to serve his whims.

Olivia by contrast is the New Woman, and her triumph over George exemplifies Milne's view that modern marriage should be a partnership and not an enslavement of wife to husband. In all of Milne's novels except *The Red House Mystery*, women are stronger, wiser, and infinitely more engaging than men. Milne's wife Daphne, who received the dedication of the volume which included the play *Mr. Pim Passes By*, inspired him with such an ideal of womanhood that even his noblest males suffer in comparison to his women. Daphne, who was charming, humorous, and forthright, was indulgent of men but not to the point of effacing her own positive and decidely attractive character; and so is Olivia. She is the New Woman but she is neither a blaring suffragette nor a cigarette-puffing Flapper; she is not free with a bottle or with her favors. She is new but also old; womanhood, eternal and unchangeable—she is strong but she veils her strength with tenderness; wise but she never flaunts her wisdom; beautiful but she does not exploit beauty to achieve her goals. Inevitably, she overshadows George, but the shadow she casts is a soft suffusion rather than a blackness, and George is illuminated rather than obliterated—inspired to his best, excused of his worst. Never raising her voice, but exercising those intuitive womanly wiles to which Barrie paid tribute in *What Every Woman Knows*, Olivia humbles her husband without wounding his pride and asserts her right to be a comrade as well as a wife. Of Olivia it is said:

She is tall, and a woman; and her voice—Yet, if she had no voice, she could speak to you forever with her eyes, and if she were blind, you could read in her finger-tips what she was thinking. She moved, and revealed the true goddess: a goddess with a sense of humor. "Devastating," said Dinah to Mr. Pim, meaning nothing by the word but that Olivia was worth waiting to see. Devastating—no. Olivia devastated no homes; she flooded them slowly with her dear beauty.[4]

The novel is, however, more than praise for a woman's charm and a plea for woman's rights. It is also an oblique assault on the outworn attitudes of the rustic aristocracy, those same folk satirized by Goldsmith in *She Stoops to Conquer* and by Fielding in *Tom Jones*. Good people, often kind, they are also proud, backward, and so set in their ways that, as in the case of George Marden, they can only be dislodged by coercion. Faced with modern art, Brian's art, George huffs, "I know what I like, and I can't see much in this new-fangled stuff." It is Olivia's task to introduce him to "new-fangled stuff" in more ways than one. She also has problems with his Aunt Julia, who, hearing that Olivia has a previous undivorced husband, is all for shipping her back to him at once and keeping the scandal out of the papers. " 'What does this mean, George?' asked his Aunt Julia sternly. 'I leave you for ten minutes, barely ten minutes, to go and look at the pigs, and when I come back you tell me that Olivia is a bigamist.' "

The same Milne who, when young, had avidly collected invitations to English country houses now punctures the traditions and pretensions of the very people who were once his hosts. His satiric shafts are nothing so clumsy as arrows, but are poison darts—small, quick, deadly, and quite deserved. Since Milne's callow days as a weekly contributor to *Punch* and a weekend partygoer, he had married a remarkable woman and fought in a remarkably disagreeable war. He had grown up to a world which was changing and had to change. He knew that it was time to reexamine the old morality and see how much of it was founded on true moral principles, and how much on arbitrarily defined manners. He may not have welcomed the future without reservations; he may have entitled the book about his youth *Those Were the Days* and have written a host of dated, drawing-room comedies in which he was more nostalgic than satiric; but in *Mr. Pim Passes By* he smiles wryly at change and holds out his hand. Olivia, who is his spokesman, says in defense of Brian, "I suppose we all have our own styles." The style of the 1920's is not that of Victoria.

The book has faults as well as virtues. The young lovers Brian and Dinah are frequent types in Milne; they are the Modern Girl and the Modern Boy whom we met in *Michael and Mary* and other plays and meet again in *Four Days' Wonder.* They exchange endearments in what is presumably intended to be a sophisticated fashion, but which strikes today's reader as a trifle fatuous:

He gave a kiss to the tips of his fingers and flicked it in her direction. She snapped it as it went past, and put it to her lips.
"Oh, well caught!"
"Now then, here's one coming for you."
It was a high dropping one, but Brian negotiated it safely. He rose and bowed.
"Madame, I thank you."
She curtsied to him.
"Your servant, sir."[5]

Perhaps the fault lies not with Milne but with the time in which he wrote; perhaps, in spite of Futurism, young people in 1921 talked and behaved with an unpalatable mixture of archness and sentiment. But today's "Lively generation" would not be caught flicking kisses from their fingertips, and Brian and Dinah must seem to them as out of date as the Charleston.

But the other characters—George, Mr. Pim, Aunt Julia, and the luminous Olivia—do not deserve to be shut in an unread book on unvisited shelves. Like genies in a bottle, they cry for the rescue of eager fingers and sympathetic laughter; cry for release into a world which still has Georges and still needs Olivias to love them out of their follies.

II   The Red House Mystery

In his introduction to *The Red House Mystery*, Milne wrote:

> When I told my agent a few years ago that I was going to write a detective story, he recovered as quickly as could be expected, but made it clear to me (as a succession of editors and publishers made it clear, later, to him) that what the country wanted from "a well-known *Punch* humorist" was a "humorous story." However, I was resolved upon a life of crime; and the result was such that when, two years afterwards, I announced that I was writing a book of nursery rhymes, my agent and my publisher were equally convinced that what the English-speaking nations most desired was a new detective story.[6]

A resounding success in 1922, *The Red House Mystery* ran through twelve printings in four years; and the inexpensive popular edition of 1936 is still sustained in print by a modest sale. In 1965, The Book-of-the-Month Club announced the book as half of a "Double Alternate" for its regular monthly selection. It was Milne's only detective novel (though *Four Days' Wonder* begins with a promise of detection which it never fulfills). In spite of popular demand and the urgings of a now converted agent and publisher, as well as the promise of an American publisher to pay Milne two thousand pounds for the serial rights to his next mystery, he never returned to the genre except in plays and short stories. Perhaps he felt that *The Red House Mystery* had perfectly illustrated his theory for such books and additional attempts in novel form would result in repetition or failure.

According to Milne's theory, (1) a detective novel should be written simply and not in formal and inflated language. He did not care for writers who said that the murderer "had effected an egress" when they could have said "gone out." (2) A detective novel should not be cluttered with romantic interludes which interrupt the solution of the crime. (3) The detective should be an amateur and not a professional; he should utilize his wits and not depend on the resources of modern science: "Away with the scientific detective, the man with the microscope!" (4) The detective should have a confidant like Holmes' Watson, to whom he may soliloquize and reveal his theories even as they develop: "Death to the author who keeps his unraveling for the last chapter, making all the other chapters but prologue to a five-minute drama."[7]

Milne, whose introductions are often better than his books, has this time written a book which justifies his introduction. *The Red House Mystery* is not, as Alexander Woollcott insisted, one of the three best mystery stories of all time. Milne is neither a Wilkie Collins nor, in spite of his admiration for Sherlock Holmes and Watson, an A. Conan Doyle. But he more than fulfills his four principles and, in the fulfillment, conceals them with the convincing artifices of fiction. In short, he has written a book sufficient in suspense and superior in characterization and scene.

Suspense, of course, is the first and absolute requisite for a successful mystery. After the crime is committed, the author must rapidly enough brandish clues before his detective and his reader to give them a sense of unfolding and development, intriguingly enough to tease them into searching for further clues, and slowly enough not to reveal the identity of the killer until the last chapter. In *The Red House Mystery*, Antony Gillingham, a gentlemanly thirty-year-old soldier of fortune who has worked to satisfy his insatiable curiosity, as a waiter, a clerk in a tobacconist shop, a valet, and a newspaper reporter, comes to the English village of Woodham for a vacation; and, finding that his old friend, Bill Beverly, is visiting at a nearby mansion, the Red House, he pays him a call. He arrives in time to find himself embroiled with Bill in a murder. It seems that the ne'er-do-well brother of the owner has arrived from Australia and been greeted by a bullet in his head, and that the owner himself, an insufferable popinjay by the name of Mark Ablett, who dabbles in literature and amateur theatricals, has mysteriously and suspiciously vanished from the neighborhood.

The police assume, and so does the reader, that Mark has quarreled with his brother, shot him, and gone into hiding. Except for Bill Beverly and Mark Ablett's cousin and personal secretary, Matthew Cayley, the house guests are cleared by the police and released to return to London; and Antony moves in to take their place, ostensibly to keep Bill company but actually to solve a murder which does not seem to him as simple as it does to the police; for there are various complications. There are secret passages to be explored and family secrets to be exposed. Working without the police and their equipment and thus fulfilling the author's insistence on an amateur and unscientific detective, and and all the while expounding his Poe-like ratiocinations to Bill, who serves as the necessary Watson, Antony deduces that the dead man is *not* the roguish brother from Australia (who actually died three years before his supposed arrival at the Red House), but that he is Mark himself in disguise; and that the murderer is Cayley, the cousin, Mark's rival in a love affair with a local belle.

Plot summaries, usually dull, are totally inadequate for *The Red House Mystery,* which, when summarized reads like a farce of mistaken identity—in fact, like one of Milne's lesser plays. But Milne generates considerable and not in the least farcical mystification as Antony and Bill chase clues and a possible corpse through a secret passageway or search a muddy lake for a bundle which may be a body. There are red herrings and additional suspects along the way—for instance, the young Miss Norbury whom both the murdered Mark and the live Cayley have loved—but, true to his four principles, Milne does not waste time on romantic interludes. His clean, swift prose—the perfect exemplification of his principle that mystery writers should write simply—hurries Antony to a solution of the crime in four concentrated days.

Suspense, however, is not the chief excellence of the book. By present-day standards, and to readers addicted to the plenitude of thrills in Ian Fleming or Daphne du Maurier, the story may seem to be uneventful and even bland. There are no sadistic Eurasians with tunnels guarded by tarantulas and giant squids, nor are there Spectre agents with poison spikes on the tips of their shoes. There are no Rebeccas threatened by housekeepers in sinister Mandalays, nor Cousin Rachels with a penchant for poisons. The only murder is mild and almost goreless. "It was not a pleasant sight," is all that Milne will tell us, in sharp contrast to what he later called "the Whiskey-Straight school of America (in which the interest centers on the number of drinks, blondes and beatings-up the 'Private Eye' can absorb in a day's induction)."[8] Exemplified by Mickey Spillane, such writers scatter gore like confetti and introduce blondes only to have them beaten up or gunned down, preferably when in the nude.

Milne's success, on the contrary, lies less in surprise or shock than in characters meticulously individualized against a convincing background. Antony is no stock detective or espionage agent. He does not resemble that featureless hero, James Bond, about whom all we know is that his face is "rather cruel" and that he would just as soon torture a woman as seduce her. Nor is Antony suave, Olympian, and equally featureless like Earle Stanley Gardner's Perry Mason, who never loses either a case or his poise. When Gardner was questioned about personal concept of Perry, he replied to an interviewer: " 'Perry?'—from the voice tone it was evident he regarded him as a living presence—'I can't tell you what he looks like. I blurred everything as much as possible, wanted the reader to create his own image. . . .' "[9]

But Milne was too scrupulous a storyteller to blur Antony. We know his background as a well-to-do young gentleman who chose adventure as some men choose security. We know that he has a memory which photographs everything he sees and holds the details like undeveloped negatives until he needs the developed prints. We know that he comes to sympathize with the murderer, who, he discovers, is much more likable than the victim, and that he warns him before alerting the police. We know his mind and his heart; he is not a shell to be possessed by the reader like an empty conch by a hermit crab. He is Antony Gillingham, soldier of fortune. Most of Milne's heroes are silken and effete, if not effeminate. A languor pervades them, the mark of the Wildan esthete, the dilettante. Men of perception instead of action, they adore rather than rival the women who stride, goddess-like, among them. Because the women are strong, compelling, and worthy of adoration, the men must sacrifice a measure of their masculinity and becomes satellites, subordinates, sychophants; eunuchs to the Mother Goddess. But Antony is a welcome exception: he is manly without being tough, an adventurer without being a ruffian.

As for Bill, the Watson of the story, Milne wrote: "A little slow let him be, as so many of us are, but friendly, human, likable." In the vast library of the Red House, the only book which interests him is an explanation of badminton. The one quotation he knows is Coleridge's famous stanza beginning, "Water, water, everywhere . . . ," and he misquotes the last line as "And not a drop to drink." He seems to spend his life bounding happily from invitation to invitation, from tennis to golf to croquet. But his

high spirits, his engaging obtuseness, are the perfect counter-
points to Antony's seriousness. When Bill learns about the secret
passage, he exclaims: "I say, what fun! I love secret passages.
Good Lord, and this afternoon I was playing golf just like an
ordinary merchant! What a life! Secret passages!" In his bumbling
enthusiasm, he resembles nothing so much as an anthropomor-
phized Pooh, whose Christopher Robin is the resourceful Antony.
When annoyed, he shouts Pooh's favorite expletive, "Bother";
and, taking a walk in the country, he might be Pooh about to
compose a hum: "he hummed to himself, hit at thistles in the
grass with his stick and made uncomfortable noises with his pipe."

Such characters do not exist in a vacuum, and part of their
credibility grows from the background in which they move: the
Red House with its pigeon-haunted elms and bee-haunted flowers; its golf links and its croquet wickets; its old-fashioned ele-
gance. It is a familiar sort of house in Milne, a little island of
eternal leisure, of sports by day and conversation or card games
by night. We have seen this setting in many of his plays, attractive in itself but sometimes tedious in its occupants, who chatter
endlessly without wit or purpose and who never seem headed
beyond the tennis court. But a country house is anything but
dull when a murder has been committed in one of its rooms. For
once, Milne has given the occupants an occupation besides wield-
ing a croquet mallet, and conversations about something besides
the latest cricket match. The tranquility of their accustomed life
accentuates for them the shock and suddenness of the crime: by
no means a monstrous crime, but one which explodes in the sleek
corridors of the Red House like a time bomb planted by Irish
terrorists and triggers in turn a highly engrossing tale. Throughout the story, the ironic contrast between the dignified mansion
and the rude murder provides a dramatic substance far more
substantial than endless quantities of blondes and beatings.

D. H. Lawrence introduced a gamekeeper into the placid life
of Lady Chatterley and shook her mansion to its moldering foundations. It lay beyond Milne's inclination or power to intrude a
Mellors into the Red House; Antony, though he has been a valet,
remains at heart the gentleman he was born and knows how to
dress for dinner. But Milne has intruded something which, in its
different way, is almost as exciting as an uninhibited gamekeeper: a corpse of mistaken identity.

III   Two People

The decade of *Winnie-the-Pooh*, of *Mr. Pim Passes By*, both
play and novel, and *The Red House Mystery* was finished; and
with 1931 came *Two People*, the first disquieting suggestion that
Milne had reached his peak in all major fields and has begun a
general decline. Admirers of *Mr. Pim* shook their heads and,
unable to foresee that four bad plays and a second bad novel
would punctuate the decade like the smudges of Roo and Tigger,
hoped that his decline was temporary; that the previous decade
of continuous and often brilliant creation had not exhausted his
powers. The failure of *Two People* was as serious as it was obvious, since, foregoing the balanced plots of his previous novels,
Milne had succumbed to the formlessness of contemporary fiction—and without the excuse of experimentation. He had written
not a bold experiment like Joyce's *Finnegans Wake* but a plotless
novel which was also conventional.

Two People is the account of an English gentleman, Reginald
Wellard, who lives contentedly with his wife, Sylvia, on a small
rustic estate until he writes the novel *Bindweed* which, in a
fashion never made clear by the author, combines horticulture
and humanity to become a critical and popular success. Now a
celebrity, Reginald moves his wife to London in order to cultivate
his new contacts in the publishing world and, since *Bindweed* is
soon adapted as a play, in the world of the theater. The contacts,
hardly sensational, lead to no consequences more dramatic than
a mild misunderstanding with Sylvia and a grateful return to
the country.

The attempts of a writer to win recognition can become the
stuff of both anguish and ecstasy, as Thomas Wolfe has shown
in *The Web and the Rock*. But anguish and ecstasy are not
Milne's intention; rather, he has tried to show the quietly telling
effects of success on the lives of the author and his wife—an un-
dertaking for which we might think him, like Henry James,
admirably suited. For was Milne not an ackowledged master of
the microcosm rather than the macrocosm, the intimate study
rather than the panorama; and, being himself both novelist and
dramatist, was he not acquainted with the world into which he had
thrust his characters? He was not attempting an intensive study
like Tolstoy's *War and Peace*, but a drawing-room serio-comedy

of limited dimensions. Even while deliberately discarding the arranged incidents which constitute a plot and which had distinguished *Mr. Pim Passes By*, he might at least have written with wit and worldliness; indeed, he might have made of his freedom from the demands of plot an opportunity to revel in scene and character, to flash epigrams and polish nuances, and to probe with Jamesian subtlety beneath the twinkling surface of success and bare an artist's soul.

But freedom to Milne proved fatal. He bares not a soul but an ego. Reginald is a blatant egotist, but without the colorful and Byronic egotism which compels even while it vexes. He is timid as well as egotistical, but without the compassion which timorous people often develop for others like themselves. He is, in fact, such an unqualified dullard that he does not seem capable of writing a bad short story, much less a celebrated novel. His one real achievement, besides his novel, is having won for his wife a beautiful and desirable woman who idolizes him; but he silently reproaches her because she does not seem impressed by his book and his fame, and because he considers her his intellectual inferior. Confronted with such a man and totally unconvinced that he possesses the talent attributed to him by Milne, or the charm attributed to him by his wife, we can hardly be interested in his few pallid adventures, the temptations from which inertia and not character protects him, and the growth and the wisdom which he fails to acquire.

It may be argued that modern heroes are rarely heroic, that many are weaklings and some are dullards. In modern criticism, the very word "hero" is often replaced by "protagonist," and the protagonists of such plays as Miller's *Death of a Salesman* and Albee's *Who's Afraid of Virginia Woolf?* are burdened with frailties and incalculably remote from Aeneas and Hector, Theseus and Hercules, as well as from the more human but no less manly Rochesters and Heathcliffs of the Victorian fiction of the Brontë sisters. But the modern hero, when not heroic, must provide a substitute for heroism, or he cannot claim our attention and justify his creation. He may win our pity like clubfooted Philip Carey in Maugham's *Of Human Bondage*. He may tickle our fancy like lecherous Humbert Humbert in Vladimir Nabokov's *Lolita*. Or, if he is purely negative, a cipher, a nonentity like the protagonist of Edward Loomis' *The Charcoal Horse*, he may pro-

vide his author with a chance for brilliantly clinical probing which
fascinates by its revelation of emptiness instead of fullness. Unhap-
pily, the protagonist of *Two People* is neither pathetic nor amusing; he is simply neutral, and Milne is less than brilliant when he
probes neutrality.

Two People is distinguished by one person, the heroine Sylvia,
who is wise, lovely, and endearing; less intelligent than Olivia in
Mr. Pim Passes By, she is, however, no less intuitive. She is one
of those radiant creatures inspired by Milne's own wife, and to
call her by the colorless word "protagonist" is to call a mermaid
a sea-cow. Sylvia indeed compels our interest because of her
beauty, her devotion to an undeserving husband, and her un-
shakable innocence when confronted by metropolitan worldliness.
But the burden of *Two People* does not rest on her ivory shoulders
but on those of a husband, who, alas, is round-shouldered.

IV Four Days' Wonder

Four Days' Wonder, published in 1933, is the weakest of all
Milne's novels and probably his worst book since *Lovers in
London*. It is one of those literary disasters which only a gifted
writer can perpetrate because the badness results in large measure from the prostitution of gifts, from an author caricaturing
his own best self. In such cases, the reader is constantly irritated
by potentialities unfulfilled, characters who are echoes, and
devices of style exaggerated into mannerisms.

The action of *Four Days' Wonder*, like that of *The Red House
Mystery*, is concentrated into a few days and in a reasonably
small area; but, in this instance concentration is synonomous
with tedium. The title refers to a certain Tuesday, Wednesday,
Thursday, and Friday which disrupt and transform the unruffled
life of the eighteen-year-old heroine, Jenny Windell, an orphan
reared by her Aunt Caroline in Auburn Lodge, the old family
home. When the story opens on Tuesday, we are told that Aunt
Caroline has recently died and that Jenny has departed from
Auburn Lodge, which is now rented by strangers, to live with
the family solicitor, the aged Mr. Watterson. But Jenny is home-
sick for the lodge; wandering in the neighborhood, she impul-
sively uses her old key to open the door and, horror of horrors,
finds on the floor the body of a woman she identifies as Caroline's

sister, Jane, whose indiscretions as a minor actress and a major sinner have long piqued the fancy of the British public. Terrified, she flees from the house, but not before touching the bronze, elephant-shaped doorstop which seems to have been the murder weapon and dropping a handkerchief with the name "Jenny" written in large letters. Fearing involvement, she decides to leave the city.

The next three days concern her adventures in the country, where she meets and falls in love with a young artist, and with the efforts of the police to find her and, having found her on the fourth day, to determine that there has not been a murder at all. It seems that Aunt Jane, who had just returned from a voyage with one of her lovers and not yet heard about Caroline's death and the rental of Auburn Lodge, had come to the house to demand money from her sister. In the absence of the new renters, she had entered, slipped on the floor, and killed herself by striking her head against the doorstop.

In synopsis, the book recalls a Nancy Drew mystery: a young girl becomes involved in a crime and finds romance and maturity. Milne, who wrote brilliantly for children, might have accomplished a lesser success for adolescents had he not committed the cardinal fault of mystery writers, even of juvenile mystery writers. Forgetting his own achievement in *The Red House Mystery*, he has written a detective story in which the "murder"—of which he pointedly remarks on the ninety-fourth page, "There was never any doubt that it was Murder"—is revealed in the last pages to have been an accident. All of the heroine's adventures are seen to have hinged on a misunderstanding. The furor has been for nothing; or rather, it has been a devious and artificial device of the author to have his heroine meet a young man who resembles Brian Strange in *Mr. Pim Passes By*, but who lacks his talent for drawing square clouds and blue sheep. Instead of an exciting denouement in which the colorful Aunt Jane is shown to have been involved in and undone by plots and machinations, we are given the casual explanation that she lost her footing and struck her head on a bronze elephant. In other words, we have been promised a detective story but given a romance.

Until the disappointing conclusion, however, Milne might at at least have held our interest and made his four days' wonder seem wonderful. Although Jenny's sweetheart is merely a copy of a dim original, Jenny herself is fetching, if a little ridiculous, as she flies from London and defends her honor against tramps and lechers with the help of a water pistol, or prays to her departed father, a one-time Hussar. There are touches of charm of the era in this virginal young girl whose experience with alcohol is limited to one cocktail and whose experience with boys does not include a kiss. Finding her aunt's body, she reacts with overtones of Pooh Bear and Alice in Wonderland: " 'Oh!' said Jenny. And then 'Well!' And then, in surprising, 'Why, it's Aunt Jane!' "—unbelievable, but naïvely appealing.

But much of the story does not belong to Jenny. Milne has intruded a subplot concerning characters who have no place in a teen-age frolic about an Alice in Wonderland heroine: the vain and worldly author Archibald deserves the satire leveled at him, but he appears to have wandered in from one of Milne's drawing-room comedies; and a calculating actress of whom it is said that "In her natural purity, as seen only be her husband and her maid, Miss Treherne looked no more than thirty. Made-up for the early twenties, to which, from her professional record, she could not possibly belong, she immediately suggested the middle forties."

It is no doubt possible to write a juvenile romp which is also a social satire, for Lewis Carroll accomplished such a feat. But Milne has failed in *Four Days' Wonder*. To belong in Jenny's book, the pompous Archibald and the painted Miss Treherne ought to be whimsical instead of sophisticated; ought to be parodied as well as pilloried. Far from providing a pungent contrast to Jenny, they get in her way. Mystery, romance, satire, farce, and peopled with naïve teen-agers and jaded sophisticates, *Four Days' Wonder* ends by resembling that clumsy hybrid among animals, the griffin. We are never sure if it will fly, lope, or crawl.

V   Chloe Marr

Chloe Marr, laid somewhat vaguely in the period between the two world wars but not published until 1946, was Milne's last novel. Better than *Two People*, much better than *Four Days' Wonder*, it is in fact, his most ambitious book, the one in which he attempted the largest scene and the greatest complexity of character. Milne's reach, however, has exceeded his grasp.

Who is Chloe Marr? Her first name has the innocent ring of a nursery rhyme or a pastoral idyll; her second name, reduced by an "r," denotes destruction. No one knows her origins, but she appears on the London social scene to hold sway over the hearts of more men than the reader (and possibly the novelist) can count. The plot of the book, or the loosely sprinkled incidents which pass for a plot, concern her relationships—half amorous, half sisterly—with an artist, Claude; an editor, Barnaby; a simpleton, Percy; a gentleman, Sir Everard; and other admirers. And Milne has set himself the task of showing her entirely through their eyes and not through her own thoughts. He tries to justify his method by making Sir Everard remark: "Have you ever noticed how little the modern novelist's habit of recording and analyzing his characters' thought helps a reader to see the character?"

But Milne must record her speech, if not her thoughts; and herein lies his first failure: he fails to make her as wittily devastating as her admirers claim. They continually marvel at her cleverness, and Everard enjoys "introducing important people to her, and seeing them fall, as instantly as had he, to her compelling conjunction of beauty and wit." But, when she speaks, as in the following conversation with Barnaby, the editor, we find no wit:

"Darling, I simply must have my bath."
"All right, ducky. Seven-twenty-five."
"Goody, goody, goody. What are you going to do now?"
"Lord's, I think."
"Enjoy yourself, sweetie. Give my love to both the umpires, and say I'm terribly happy because I'm going out with my best boy tonight...."[10]

Chloe, it must be admitted, is not always fatuous. She can hold her own in discussions of art and drama, and she is quick to recognize a literary allusion. With the Vicar of Much Hadingham, she shows herself such a perceptive heretic that he prefers her to most of his pious flock. Certainly, too, her physical beauty is unquestionable. In the words of Barnaby: "She's more beautiful than ever, but I mustn't be a fool about it, she's just something beautiful like bluebells in a wood, or *Primavera*, or the 'Ode to a Nightingale,' they are yours but you don't own them, and they don't break your heart."

But far too often Milne forsakes his at least intermittently attractive heroine for his multitudinous heroes, who have as many friends and relations as Rabbit in *Winnie-the-Pooh*. There is nothing incongruous about these multitudes in the context of the story; unlike the too sophisticated author and actress in *Four Days' Wonder*, they never appear to have wandered into the wrong book. But they are much too numerous for a novel of three hundred pages. Milne's intention is clear: he is trying to show that, to each of her lovers, Chloe is a beautiful but insubstantial phantom who can never be possessed, and that each of them, in a world designed for people and not for phantoms, must seek more substantial companions. Though the point is valid, the story does not so much develop as proliferate; and the reader must constantly turn back the pages to identify Chloe's escort for the evening: the artist, the editor, the simpleton,the gentleman . . .?

The weaknesses of the book are emphasized rather than redeemed by the conclusion. Chloe dies in a plane crash with a mysterious and menacing Lord Sheppey, who has previously been introduced only as a man to whom she was never at home. The question of her origin is not answered by her death. Was Sheppey (her maid Ellen wonders) the father of a hypothetical illegitimate son? Just before the crash, had he agreed to marry her and give their son—if indeed they had such a child—a name? We are never told. In posing a mystery without an answer, Milne has joined the tradition of Frank Stockton's "The Lady or the Tiger?" and, more recently, of Daphne du Maurier's "The Birds" and *My Cousin Rachel*. In the best stories of the genre, concealment is made to seem a higher art than revelation; the reader prefers to be teased by uncertainties than satisfied with solutions. But Milne has failed even to tease. Had he made his heroine more consistently attractive, a little more revealed or more artfully unrevealed, had he made her companions less numerous and less forgettable, he might have achieved a du Maurier ending.

As it is, Chloe's death seems a weak conclusion to an uneven book, and Milne's last novel is the ultimate evidence that he was a good novelist only when he imposed upon himself the traditional restrictions of a tightly constructed plot. As the book critic for *Time* wrote: "Readers who know A. A. Milne as the creator of whimsical juveniles and endearing animals are likely to be rocked back on their heels when they open *Chloe Marr*,

Author Milne's first novel for adults in 13 years. . . . Pooh is the word for Chloe Marr."[11] In an era of bold experiment and sometimes inspired formlessness, Milne's best novels, *Mr. Pim Passes By* and *The Red House Mystery*, are his well-made novels.

CHAPTER 8

Bagatelles

VERSATILITY was a mixed blessing to Milne. For every writer there are crests of exhausting creation which ought to be followed by troughs of rest and recovery. Milne, however, did not like to rest. No sooner did he establish himself as an essayist than he hurried to write a play. Established as a dramatist, he turned to novels and juveniles. His four major careers sometimes complemented each other, but they also at times conflicted, drawing him in several directions at once, sapping his creativity, producing repeated failures along with memorable successes. As an additional drain on his powers, he also wrote three volumes of poems and three volumes of short stories. In neither of these areas can he be said to have carved an additional career—his offerings are too infrequent and undistinguished; they are afterthoughts, bagatelles. Some of his poems and stories have the look of beautiful women who have suffered the visitation of vampires: they are shapely of form but pale and very anemic. Others have the look of vampires after the visitation: overstuffed with undigested materials.

I *The Poems*

Milne's earliest poetry was not a by-product of his prose. In fact, he became a poet at the age of seventeen, when he went home from Westminster to spend the Christmas holidays with his parents and found two young girls in the house. Their mother and father had gone to India and left them temporarily with the Milnes. The older girl, who was fourteen at the time, aspired to be a poetess. Young Milne helped her polish some awkward verses, and then he composed an ode to her ten-year-old sister, Irma, of which the only surviving lines read:

> They say the Dutch prefer their ladies short
> And fat as fat can be, but not as clean as
> Is usual here. Out there, dear, you'd be thought
> A Venus.[1]

Even if Irma did not approve the verses, Milne found a willing audience in his brother Ken; and the boys began a collaboration which lasted for two years and climaxed in a six-line form called the "Milnick," a kind of elongated limerick. Scorned by *Punch*, they published their verses in Alan's school magazine, *The Elizabethan*, under the initials of A. K. M. (Alan and Ken Milne). When Alan went to Cambridge and his verse began to appear without Ken's collaboration in the *Granta*, he had grown so attached to initials that he signed himself "A. A. M.," and then "A. A. Milne." For the rest of his life, readers conjectured at the "Alan Alexander" concealed behind the cryptic "A. A."

After he had left Cambridge and gone to London, however, he wrote for a livelihood and not for recreation. Since poetry was less remunerative than prose, he began his career as an essayist, and the poems he continued to write were few in number and similar to the essays which he called his "light articles." His principal market for the poems was *Punch;* his subjects were those which inspired the essays—a cricket match ("Hymn on Tomkins' Action"), the trials of an uncle ("To Jock"), a card game ("Poets at Bridge"). Even the title of his first collection, *For the Luncheon Interval* (1925), is akin in lightness and frivolity to those of his five collections of *Punch* essays, *The Day's Play, Once a Week, The Holiday Round, The Sunny Side,* and *Those Were the Days.* Unfortunately, the poems also resemble the essays in their weaknesses: their labored and bloodless trivialities.

It is, to be sure, an author's privilege to write verses for the "luncheon interval" instead of the lecturer's podium. Some of the Christopher Robin poems, designed for that child's equivalent to the luncheon interval, the hour before bed, are trifles exalted to classics because the author, though taking his craft with utmost seriousness, relaxed with his subjects. John and his macintosh are not exactly the materials for an epic, but they provide a vignette of a little boy in the rain which is all the jollier for seeming as spontaneous as the falling drops. Milne is not exploiting the boy as a subject; he is being the boy. But in his poems for adults, he has worked too hard at appearing not to have done so. As in his early essays, his art becomes artfulness. Milne fails to achieve playfulness because of his frantic efforts to seem playful.

In "Poets at Bridge," he imagines Whitman, Tennyson, Browning, and Wordsworth gathered over a table for a game of cards. In one of his plays, *Before the Flood,* he takes an irreverent and amusing look at dignified Noah. His "look" makes nothing of the four great poets, not even effective fun, but he might have individualized and lampooned them by magnifying qualities for which they were known in life—Browning's foppery, Whitman's booming exuberance, Wordsworth's predilection for finding sermons in brooks, or Tennyson's sensitivity to criticism. But he makes them indistinguishable except in their names. He seems to have written a poem about an ordinary bridge game and then, calculating the meagre number of laughs evoked by his lines, superimposed the names of famous men with the hope that recognition would evoke additional laughter. "Poets at Bridge" is typical of the volume: he has crowded too much furniture, and none of it very distinctive, into cramped and airless rooms.

His next book of verse for adults *Behind the Lines* did not appear until 1940; and the intervening years had made of the author an international—and decidedly solvent—fixture in the field of children's literature, and also brought the world to a second global war. *Behind the Lines,* dedicated to Christopher Robin, "mathematical scholar at Trinity" who was soon to join the Royal Air Force, and written during the opening nine months of the war, was reviewed with respect but without enthusiasm. As *The New York Herald-Tribune* reviewer wrote: "Mr. Milne is unquestionably sincere and articulate. These verses, to be sure, are not distinguished, and even their palpable sincerity, and the poignancy of some of the situations they record, cannot make them so. . . ."[2] Milne, who was now living at Catchford Farm in Hartfield and whose sole connection with the war was to house an occasional batch of refugees, was not equal to his task of interpreting blitzkriegs and bombings from behind the lines. He lacked the bitter savagery of Siegfried Sassoon and the passionate involvement of Wilfred Owen. Milne, attacking Hitler and Mussolini with the mosquito pricks of satire, buzzed valiantly but to little purpose; and, when he chose to be not satiric but serious, he managed only to be sentimental.

He is more convincing when he treats the effects of the war on his own life. In "Farewell to Butter" he weaves a pleasant fantasy about a swallow who sings a sea chanty to a cow—just such a cow as Christopher Robin had counted—and inspires the animal to give milk from which salty, "sea-tanged" butter used to be churned. But where, the poet sighs, are the butters of yesteryear? His answer is uncomplaining, if a little wistful: rationing has melted them, at least from his own larder. Again in "Spring Offensive," a title doubtless suggested by Wilfred Owen, Milne wryly but readily admits that he is less skillful at treating spring on the battlefield than the coming of the season to his garden, and he proves his point with horticultural charm in lieu of martial vigor. All in all, *Behind the Lines* is unarguable proof of Milne's patriotism and his willingness to write for his country if he could not fight for her. Like Edna St. Vincent Millay in *Make Bright the Arrows* and *The Murder of Lidice*, Milne wielded verses instead of weapons. But, again like Miss Millay, he wrote with the obvious air of preferring the Muse even while serving Mars, and both suffered a decline in their poetic reputations.

Milne's final volume of verse was not a collection but a long single poem, *The Norman Church* (1948), the kind of book which publishers accept only out of deference to a writer who has supplied them through many years with better, more marketable books in other fields. A philosophical poem which describes his view of religion in 981 lines, divided into 109 stanzas, this weak verse is the metaphysical equivalent of his pamphlet of 1928, *The Ascent of Man*. He accepts the existence of a God but argues that men have misconceived and grossly distorted Him. Every age encrusts Him with additional myths and also preserves the myths and misconceptions of earlier ages. The resulting deity is sometimes ludicrous, sometimes monstrous:

> To whom ascribe the kindly thought
> That babies dying unbaptized
> Were damned in Hell? Was God surprised
> To hear that this was what Himself had authorized?[3]

How, Milne asks, can we recover the original and admirable God? By rejecting the mythologies, the encrustations of the ages, even those legends sanctified by inclusion in the Bible, and by comprehending God through our search for knowledge and especially through His manifestations in nature: "In each new miracle of birth/God is enthroned again on earth. . . ."[4] Though we may not be allowed to spend eternity with Him in heaven, we should make our lives on earth a fullness and a fulfillment.

There is nothing bold or original in Milne's philosophy. The preceding century—the era of Charles Darwin, Thomas Huxley, and Herbert Spencer—had stridently and repeatedly questioned a literal interpretation of the Bible, and Milne has, therefore, raised and answered no questions which would have surprised Tennyson. But lack of originality need not be a fault in a philosophical poem; indeed poets who write such poems are rarely original. Lucretius went to the Greeks, to Democritus and Epicurus, for the mechanism and epicureanism of *On the Nature of Things;* Alexander Pope, when he wrote *An Essay on Man,* acknowledged a debt to the Deism of Lord Bolingbroke; and the doubts which Tennyson expressed with *In Memoriam* were those of his troubled century. But Lucretius, Pope, and Tennyson, in spite of their debt, achieved great poems.

Milne, however, has not achieved a great or even a competent poem. The first of the four divisions, which concerns a likable vicar who is content to teach the old platitudes without questioning them, is the best; the portrait of the vicar and the Norman-style church in which he preaches are drawn with the apt colloquialism of a John Betjeman; but the following three divisions are notably less successful. Milne's forte is for people and places: for the human, not the cosmic. As soon as he departs from the vicar and the church and proceeds to question the accumulating legends and lies which have come to distort God, he departs from competence. It is not that he loses himself in the great vistas of history, in speculations concerning the fierce Yahweh and the misunderstood Christ. Rather, he treats such monumental subjects with the same directness, literalness, and casualness as he has treated the vicar. He lacks the largeness of expression or concept which large poetic themes demand, as well as the surprise and passion, the sweep and profundity. He lacks the grandeur, the resonance, and the verbal symphonics of Lucretius,

Pope, and Tennyson. His jingling verses, his nine-line stanzas of three couplets and a triplet, are suitable to the unpretentious portrait of the vicar and his "accidental village," but they cannot sustain the burden of major themes. The latter tinkle when they ought to reverberate.

Poetry about grand subjects does not have to possess a Tennysonian grandeur. Hilda Doolittle encompasses a convincing fusion of paganism and Christianity in the simple free verses of *The Walls Do Not Fall* and of *The Flowering of the Rod*. But her verses, though simple, do not jingle, and her simplicity conceals a largeness of knowledge and a boldness of concept. The poet of *The Norman Church*, on the other hand, has attempted a philosophical poem whose only value is biographical: it reveals the personal religion of a popular and respected writer.

II *The Short Stories*

The Secret and Other Stories (1929), published in a limited edition of 742 copies to be divided between England and America, is notable for its brevity but not its quality. Two of the four stories concern World War I. The soldier and titular hero of "Mullins" is a spiritualist who renders himself invulnerable on the battlefield with the walking stick of a dead friend: undeterred by a shower of bullets, he strides up to a German machine gunner, whacks him on the head with the stick, and captures the nest. The soldier in "The Return" is a clerk who goes to war, fights honorably, and returns to England expecting a partnership with his former boss, a literary agent, only to find the position filled by an unprepossessing fellow whose bad health has kept him out of the army. Like the early playlet *The Boy Comes Home*, both stories reaffirm the fact that Milne wrote lamely when he wrote about war. There is nothing objectionable in either story; there is nothing memorable. The war is a shadowy background for the characters, and not a shaping force which molds or breaks them; it is an interruption, not a holocaust.

The essential Milne, both the best and the worst of him, is also absent from "End of the Peer of Wotherspoon," the tale of a critic who exalts an unknown novelist to fame and finds himself attacked by other novelists for presenting them with a rival. Only the title story, "The Secret," a wise little fairy tale for adults,

represents Milne at his best: Milne the magician, who conjured
Pooh from Christopher Robin's nursery, opened the Ivory Door,
and renovated Toad Hall. The heroine is Princess Elvira, whose
insolence matches her beauty until, riding in the forest, she
encounters Simon, a young woodcarver who treats her as his
equal. He refuses to rise; he refuses to bow; he smiles and continues to carve. Furious, she threatens to have him killed; then
she falls furiously in love with him, renounces her pride along
with her palace, and goes to the woods to share his humble cottage. But, unlike the hero and the heroine of *The Ivory Door*,
who found the courage to live without legends, she clings to the
secret fancy that Simon is not really a woodcarver but a prince
in disguise. In other words, it is easier for her to give up palaces
than illusions.

One wise fairy tale, however, and three indifferent stories
hardly appear to justify a separate edition, even a limited one.
But Milne, who later regretted *The Secret and Other Stories* and
retained only "The Secret" for his next collection, explains that
in 1929 he had "a transitory bibliography value, a value enhanced
on this occasion by the distinction of the company which I kept
and the clothes in which I was dressed."[5] In short, the celebrated
and fashionable author of *Winnie-the-Pooh* could probably have
written a rhymed grocery list entitled "Breakfast for a Bear" or
"Christopher Robin and the Luncheon Interval" and seen it
printed on vellum and bound between leather covers.

It was nineteen years before Milne reprinted "The Secret" in
his second and better collection of stories, *Birthday Party* (1948).
To "The Secret" he added "The General Takes off His Helmet,"
an adaptation of a ten-minute duologue published in *The Queen's
Red Cross Book* at the start of World War II; "In Vino Veritas"
and "The Shakespearean Theory," which had been written for
and published in *The Saturday Book;* and eleven stories composed in 1947 and 1948 expressly for the new collection.

The stories in *Birthday Party* range from farce to fantasy, from
mystery to history; and the writing is smoothly accommodated to
the several moods and styles. The authentic hallmark of Milne—
the mingling of lightness, sentiment, charm, whimsy, and idealism
which in *Winnie-the-Pooh* and *Mr. Pim Passes By* is as unmistak-
able as a pawprint left by the Bear of Very Little Brain—is not
always in evidence. It is evident in the sentiment which is not

sentimental of "Tristram," the story of an English colonel who loses his son in World War II but who finds that sharing his memory with a crippled old lady helps to keep Tristram alive for both of them. It is evident in that sly jest, "The Shakespearean Theory." Did Bacon write Shakespeare's plays? No, we are told in the bard's own diary; Shakespeare wrote Bacon's essays.

But too often the stories might have been written by Milne's favorite authors. In "Anne-Marie," a great magician is overshadowed by his female assistant, who cuts capers in the midst of his most exalted tricks and who, when he hopes he has exorcised her, is reincarnated as the scene-stealing rabbit of the title. We think at once of Saki, whom Milne applauded in an early essay and whose classic fantasy, "Laura," concerns a woman reincarnated as an otter. Then there is "In Vino Veritas," a thriller about a drunken police inspector who confesses a poisoning to a writer of detective stories. The writer listens with fascination until he realizes that the inspector, when he is sober, will regret his damning confession and takes steps to silence his confessor. It is a chilling story, but Milne's own publisher proclaims it a "De Maupassant thriller." Milne's adaptability sometimes worked against him. He worshiped Barrie and echoed him in *Make-Believe;* he idolized Wilde and echoed him in *Belinda*. The fact that he read and loved innumerable books inevtitably tempted him to imitate innumerable authors.

He is guilty of other failures in *Birthday Party*. In "Breitenstein" he builds an intriguing mystery around a young man who meets a mysterious French woman on a train and sees her home, only to see her murdered before his eyes and laid out beside the corpse of her brother. But the murder is never solved. At the end of the story, the young man, now old, says to the unidentified listener to whom he has told the story: "I'm sorry, dear boy, but that's really all. . . . Nobody was ever arrested." The author, through his narrator, is confessing his inability to reach a satisfying conclusion. All in all, *Birthday Party* is considerably less than a feast. The guests are attractive but hardly stimulating, and the cake is a little stale beneath its pretty icing.

The thirteen stories collected in *A Table Near the Band* (1950) reaffirm the truth of *Birthday Party* that Milne as a short-story teller is agreeable and usually forgettable. In the space of two years, he has neither improved nor declined. There is a diverting tale called "The Rise and Fall of Mortimer Scrivens," told in the form of letters, about the consequences of book borrowing when the lender is a contankerous old skinflint who loves to put matters in the hands of his solicitor. There are no fewer than three murder mysteries, of which one, "Murder at Eleven," is good, and one, "Portrait of Lydia," is superior. There is the nostalgic reminiscence of a middle-aged woman who used to be, and to her husband remains, "The Prettiest Girl in in the Room."

There are also failures or partial failures. "The Three Dreams of Mr. Findlater" recounts the elaborate scheme of a plain, middle-aged Milquetoast to murder his domineering wife. But he never succeeds, nor does he even make the attempt; she suffers a timely stroke and saves him the trouble. This kind of highly convenient and wildly coincidental conclusion, once designated the "O. Henry twist," has come to be called the "Hitchcock twist," in honor or dishonor of the famous Alfred.

"Before the Flood," though vividly peopled with men and women who achieve the difficult feat of seeming both biblical and modern, can never decide if it wishes to be farcical or serious; and its people, the humorous Noah, his simple-minded wife, their ill-assorted sons and daughters-in-law, because of their very vividness, tug at the reader from opposite directions, like circus performers who want to be watched and cheered in three rings at the same time. We only wonder how Milne has resisted the urge to parade Noah's animals before our eyes. The twenty-four pages of the story are insufficient to encompass materials which the following year supplied the author with a more successful one-act play and might still better have supplied him with a novel.

Considered together, *The Secret and Other Stories, Birthday Party*, and *A Table Near the Band* may be categorized and mildly approved by the adjective "incidental." In the 1920's Milne's stories were incidental to his plays, novels and juveniles. In the late 1940's, when he turned in earnest to the writing of stories, he had passed his prime. At his rare best, he remained a first-rate raconteur like the Milne of *The Ivory Door*, a purveyor of curious plots and arresting people. At his frequent worst, he spoke with a firm voice and assured gestures but without the power and inventiveness which belong to the masters; and his tales seemed decorated incidents rather than fully realized stories.

CHAPTER 9

Back to the Bear

A. A. MILNE was a happy man but a misplaced writer; a belated Victorian who championed women's rights and eventually approved the atom bomb, he would rather have been the contemporary of Lewis Carroll than of Ernest Hemingway. He disliked both the subject matter and the techniques of most modern literature. With an eye no doubt to writers like Dreiser and Hemingway, he protested the excessive Realism, sometimes considered as Naturalism, which dominated writing in the twentieth century. He asked "why realism in a novel is so much admired when realism in a picture is condemned as mere photography," and "why drink and fornication should seem to bring the realist closer to real life than, say, golf and gardening."[1]

Nor did he approve of formlessness and bizarre typography. In his collection of short stories, *A Table Near the Band,* he ridicules experimental writers like James Joyce: "Mr. Withers had written three other novels, each of them more disordered than the one before. To the old-fashioned reader they suggested an almost illegible, much corrected first pencil draft, which had been pulled together with a '*stet* everything,' and handed over to a typist whose six easy lessons had not taken her up to capital letters and punctuation marks."[2] As for modern poetry, he complained that it was only the light versifiers who still took pains to polish and clarify, for serious poets hurried their first drafts into print and made a virtue of being unintelligible. To illustrate his point, Milne wrote a parody called "Spring in Alicante":

> Steam-hammers like white thoughts clanking
> as once (once)
> "as once" in Nanking
> once in months the visceral bull
> target-centered enters
> papal, palpable,

China-town, China-town, China-town
crockery and mockery
Thighs dew-ridden in the pastoral yoke
egg-white rag-red
steam-hammers
pulsing and repulsing equal and opposite
Ice.[3]

Milne's objections to the modern manner were often valid and
always articulate, and he was exercising a writer's privilege when
he chose to remain a traditionalist, with Lamb, Wilde, and Barrie
for his guiding masters. But it is one thing to be guided; it is
another to be dominated. The traditionalist is not expected to
lead a revolution, but he ought to enrich the existing order—and
enrichment is not the same as repetition. Milne has heroines
whom he seems to have lifted, fully costumed and spouting
epigrams, from Oscar Wilde, and entire plays which read like
rejected drafts by Barrie. Though Milne was adventurous enough
to explore a number of forms—today, an essay; tomorrow, a play
—he sometimes so zealously hugged the trails blazed by his prede-
cessors and so successfully avoided the lions and rhinoceroses
of innovation that he seems less a hunter armed with an elephant
gun than a tourist with camera and guidebook.

Furthermore, he sometimes fails in his own right and not
through imitation. At his worst, he is not second-rate Barrie or
Wilde but second-rate Milne. Most of his early essays are simpering trivialities. Most of his drawing-room plays, both light and
serious, creak with wooden heroes and cardboard heroines; and
the Modern Girls who, brandishing cigarettes and highballs,
saunter across his stage and announce an engagement as if it
were for cocktails instead of marriage, seem more outlandish than
modern. His short stories rarely achieve the significance they
attempt; two of his novels are bores and a third is unbelievable
as well as boring; and the Mars who inspired his war poems was
either emasculated or enervated. As Frank Swinnerton wrote of
him: "Although by no means unappreciative of these traits in
other men, he is deficient in vulgarity, in energy, in largeness of
thought, and in exuberance of action."[4]

Fortunately, time has been kind to Milne; it has killed the
worst of his books. Devotees of Shakespeare still feel obliged to
read *Titus Andronicus*, but devotees of Milne have already been

relieved of *Lovers in London* and *Four Days' Wonder*. True, time has also obscured a deserving novel like *Mr. Pim Passes By* and some excellent fairy-tale plays. But *By Way of Introduction, Year In, Year Out, The Red House Mystery, Toad of Toad Hall,* and *Once on a Time* are accessible if not celebrated, while his four Winnie-the-Pooh and Christopher Robin books burgeon in manifold editions and sell in "large and ridiculous quantities." When all is said, of course, the four children's books represent Milne to the public and constitute his claim to a warm and unassailable niche in the children's corner of English literature. He often protested his niche: "No artist but hates to be pinned in a groove like a dead and labeled butterfly, and none of the secular but loves so to pin him, feeling that thus, and thus only, is he safe."[5] But a butterfly, unless he is pinned and labeled, may expect a life span of a few weeks; and then, shredded by buffeting winds and devoured by ants, he becomes effaced into the garden which once sustained him. For authors, especially dead authors, there is much to be said for pins and labels.

In part, Milne has earned his label with his meticulous yet natural style. As a stylist, he felt that children as well as adults deserved balanced sentences and musical verses. Perhaps the very young would overlook an awkward phrase or a wrenched rhyme, but Milne wrote first of all to satisfy his own exacting conscience: "A 'children's book' must be written, not for children, but for the author himself.... Whatever fears one has, one need not fear that one is writing too well for a child, any more than one need fear that one is becoming almost too lovable. It is difficult enough to express oneself with all the words in the dictionary at one's disposal; with none but simple words the difficulty is much greater. We need not spare ourselves."[6] It can be said of him that, thanks to the niceties of his style, children enjoy the sound of his books as well as the sense, and parents who grow exasperated with the inelegant and graceless sentences of *Uncle Wiggily* linger on the elegances of a dialogue between Pooh and Piglet.

Subject, however, is even more important than style in a children's book. In some of his Christopher Robin poems, in parts of *Once on a Time,* but especially in his books about Pooh, Milne enlarges and enhances a long tradition: that of the beast fabulist who lends to animals the characteristics of men—clothes, speech, mannerisms—and engages them in various amusing or instructive adventures. The earlier fabulists, from antiquity through the middle years of Queen Victoria's reign, amused in order to instruct: Aesop and Ovid; Chaucer, Fontaine, and Swift; Charles Kingsley. Some of their beasts have joined the great menagerie of world literature: the fox who cried sour grapes; Pertelote, the foolish hen; those talking horses with unspellable names, the Houyhnhnms. But the authors had preachment in mind as well as amusement: their animals, however delightful, are walking lessons. Even that charming tale of chimney sweeps and sea animals, Kingsley's *The Water Babies*, ends with the blatant advice: "Meanwhile, do your lessons, and thank God that you have plenty of cold water to wash in; and wash in it too,'like a true Englishman. And then, if my story is not true, something better is; and if I am not quite right, still you will be, as long as you stick to hard work and cold water."

In 1862, however, a mathematics don named C. L. Dodgson, better known as Lewis Carroll, took a memorable boat ride on the Thames with three little girls and began the stories which became *Alice in Wonderland* (1865) and *Through the Looking Glass* (1871). There is certainly truth in Carroll—sense disguised as nonsense; logic concealed behind illogicalities—but his readers are rarely conscious of being taught. His white rabbits and dormice, his impudent snails and fearsome Jabberwockys, inhabit the very forests of Aesop and Fontaine, but the forests have become playgrounds instead of classrooms; they serve for delectation instead of education.

Carroll's contemporary, Edward Lear, reveled in the now liberated tradition and sent his Owl and Pussy-Cat to sea in a "beautiful pea-green boat." In America, Joel Chandler Harris collected and revised old Negro folk tales about Bre'r Rabbit and Bre'r Fox into the Uncle Remus stories, which Milne's father read to his three fascinated sons. After the turn of the century, Beatrix Potter sent Peter Rabbit scurrying through Farmer McGregor's forbidden garden; Kenneth Grahame terrorized the country adjoining the Wild Woods with Mr. Toad and his motor car; Frank Baum's Dorothy encountered a timid lion on the road to Oz; and Hugh Lofting introduced that kindly veterinarian, Dr. Doolittle, and dispatched him to Africa in the company of Gub-Gub and other animal friends to trap a Pushmo-Pullow.

Milne joined these writers in placing amusement before instruction, and he spoke for all of them when he remarked of *Aunt Judy's Magazine*, which he read as a child: "She entranced us, but never told us how to make a tricycle."[7]

But Milne as a beast fabulist, though he wrote to delight and not to instruct, is neither a Carroll, nor a Lofting, nor a Grahame; and his strongest claim to uniqueness, to the individuality which is genius, lies in a single creation: Pooh. In Winnie-the-Pooh he has created his greatest character and given to literature its most beloved bear. Through the 1920's and 1930's, the Christopher Robin books were Milne's best sellers, but Pooh has eclipsed his master and *The New York Times Children's Books Section* of May 9, 1965, reported that *Winnie-the-Pooh*, thirty-nine years after its first appearance, held ninth place on a list of best sellers for children. To the modern child, Christopher Robin is not without his charm, but he is puzzling and even a little girlish. Pooh, however, merrily epitomizes the indolent meanderings, the vagrant fancies, the unassuageable appetite, and the sheer lovability of little boys. Once he was Christopher Robin's alter ego; now he belongs to every child who is friendly with Bears.

Pooh lies on his back under a honey tree, dreaming of snacks; and his eyelids creep down like snails to shut out distracting sights and to shut in his honied thoughts. He challenges anyone to take him seriously, and yet like all great clowns—Falstaff, Don Quixote, and the rest—he excites pathos as well as laughter: in his love for Christopher Robin, in his valiant if fitful efforts to serve and please him, in his touching gratitude for his master's praise, or again in his planning to take Eeyore a jar of honey for his birthday, his eating the honey en route, but his presenting the empty jar with such good fellowship that it seems the princeliest of gifts. For Pooh is more than a foolish bumbling bear; he is also thoughtful and kind; and in his kindness and in that of his friends—fond, fearful Piglet, solicitous Kanga, and the rest—the Pooh books, avoiding as they do explicit morals, are nonetheless moral: they do not teach the child's mind, but educate his heart, the highest and much the most difficult form of education. To know Pooh is to laugh at him and also to grow more loving with him.

Currently disporting himself in *Pooh's Library, Pooh: His Art Gallery, The Pooh Song Book, The Christopher Robin Story*

Book, *The Colorful Land of Pooh and Christopher Robin, Pooh's Birthday Book, The World of Pooh,* and the recent *Pooh Story Book* with new illustrations in color by the aged but still active Shepard, Pooh has passed into the cultural heritage of all English-speaking people, to say nothing of having been translated into eighteen other languages, among them Latin. In fact, as *Winnie ille Pu,* dressed like a Roman general and supported by that stalwart legionary, Piglet, he has become required reading for many Latin classes; and, in spite of carpings by purists like Gilbert Highet, who complained about vulgarized diction the translation makes highly pleasurable reading for scholars, teachers, and multilingual laymen. In his recent autobiography, *The Valley of the Latin Bear* (1965), Alexander Leonard explains how his long and affectionate acquaintance with Milne's bear inspired him to translate *Winnie-the-Pooh* into what he called "Erasmic Latin"—the Latin of the fifteenth- and sixteenth-century humanists.

During World War II, Leonard was a highly educated but penurious refugee from Hungary, who eked out a bleak existence in Venice by teaching foreign languages. When the Allies invaded Italy, the leader of the Venetian Resistance, Pietro Ferarro, came to Leonard and announced that he wished to learn English in order to negotiate for arms with the Allies. Leonard chose for his text the only English book in his possession, *Winnie-the-Poh.* "We started," he wrote, "with the chapter on the Heffalump, as I held the conversation between Pooh and Piglet as essential, in case my friend made contact with senior officers." In a few weeks Ferraro had sufficiently mastered English to meet the Allies and ask for the necessary equipment and support. Parachuted back into Venice, he led an insurrection against the Germans which kept them from sabotaging the city before their retreat. "So *Winnie-the-Pooh* had helped Winnie Churchill to win the war."[8]

But not until after the war, when Leonard had moved to Brazil and become the underpaid physician to a French mining company, did he think of a Latin translation. When two of the engineers engaged him to teach their daughters English and Latin, he selected *Winnie-the-Pooh* for his English text. The girls were enthusiastic. "Is there no Latin book like *Winnie-the-Pooh?*" one of them asked. Hesitating to recommend Petronius or Apuleius, he produced *Winnie ille Pu.* The girls applauded his efforts and learned Latin, but publishers were less responsive. In fact, he received such replies as, "Maybe you have too much spare time, but we have not" or "I am not crazy."[9] Discouraged but still determined to see his book to press, he engaged a Brazilian printer to print a hundred copies which Leonard mailed to friends, Classicists, and librarians. One of the copies went to the Royal Danish Librarian, who wrote in reply: "Winnie is known and loved in Sweden under the name of Nalle. The great Swedish publishing house Svenska Bokforlaget has decided to accept your Latin version which I submitted to them."[10] When English and American publishers followed the example of Sweden, *Winnie ille Pu* became an international publishing sensation and one more tribute to the imperturbable bear.

An even greater tribute to Pooh's celebrity—to the fact that his name is known to all literature people—is Frederick C. Crews's *The Pooh Perplex* (1963), a satire on modern criticism in which Dr. Crews, dividing himself into twelve imaginary critics, examines Pooh from the viewpoint of a Marxist, an Angry Young Man, a Freudian, a New Critic, and Esthete, and others. The twelve pieces are presented in the form of a freshman casebook; and, with elaborate seriousness, students are exhorted to read and analyze them. The Marxist, Martin Tempralis by name, claims in "A Bourgeois Writer's Proletarian Fables" that "Rabbit is the capitalist manager par excellence, the 'captain of industry' who, though altogether a bungler and boaster, is bent upon imposing his will on everyone around him. . . . Rabbit, having deceitfully offered Pooh admittance to sample his overstocked larder, artfully traps his victim in the doorway and exploits him as an unsalaried towel rack for an entire week."[11] The Angry Young Man, Myron Masterson in "Poisoned Paradise," complains that Pooh "is tragically fixated at the narcissistic stage of development. Rabbit and Owl are aging bachelors whose respective megalomania and fussiness are tempered only by their mutual friendship, of which the less said, the better. Kanga is the archetypal mawkish 'Mom'-figure we see exemplified everywhere in America."[12]

But other critics hurry to Pooh's defense and find his books analogous to *Ulysses* and a distant influence on *Finnegans Wake.* Writes Woodbine Meadowlark, the Esthete: "There are few

stories, whether written for adults or for children, more poign-
antly affecting than *Winnie-the-Pooh*. I remember how, at the age
of seven, my Aunt Amelia slipped a copy of the book into my
little hands and, with a smile that perhaps betrayed a suppressed
tear for the lost beauties of childhood, said, 'Woodbine, you will
read many a book before your time is over, for you are an
aesthetic child; but you will never read anything one-eighth so
moving as *Winnie-the-Pooh*.' "[13]

Pooh's fame, of course, is more than literary. He has not been
caged between the covers of two small books. In 1951, his battered original from Christopher Robin's nursery, together with
Piglet, Eeyore, Kanga, and Tigger, visited America and, insured
with his friends for $50,000, commenced a triumphant tour of
libraries and bookstores. Now they are sumptuously housed in
the New York offices of Milne's American publisher, E. P. Dutton and Company, and are proudly displayed to visitors of all
ages. Stuffed replicas, based on the Shepard illustrations rather
than the somewhat moth-eaten and woebegone toys which inspired them, sell in many large department stores. It is possible
to buy a place mat with Pooh in various stages of licking a honey
pot, and a matching tapestry to hang on the wall of a kitchen or
a nursery. Together with Christopher Robin, Pooh has been
sculptured in stone as a garden ornament, and the sculptor has
caught him in a rare pensive mood when he seems to be contemplating Heffalumps instead of dinner. Maurice Evans has recorded two albums of readings such as "Eeyore Loses a Tail,"
"The Heffalump," and "Winnie-the-Pooh Goes Hunting." In the
fall of 1965, Sears Roebuck introduced a Pooh style of clothes for
children, including "shaggy bear" pullovers and "bear-brown"
toggle coats with hoods of "balloon-red" and "honey-beige"; and
in the winter of 1966 Walt Disney climaxed twenty years of ne-
gotiating for film rights and released an effectively animated
but ineffectively dubbed short feature, *Winnie-the-Pooh and the
Honey Tree*, with songs by the Sherman brothers, who wrote the
music for *Mary Poppins*.

It is true that Pooh has his enemies. From his first appearance
in print, a sophisticated minority has failed to appreciate him.
They see him as a sentimentalized rather than a lovable bear,
and in the interests of Realism, they would doubtless prefer that

he have the disposition of a grizzly, a fishlike smell, and a bad case of mange, that Piglet wallow in a trough, and that Tigger maraud instead of bounce. But Milne proved a highly effective counsel for defense. When Dorothy Parker, writing as "Constant Reader" in *The New Yorker*, announced that by the fifth page of *The House at Pooh Corner*, "Tonstant Weader fwowed up," the author answered that "No writer of children's books says gaily to his publisher, 'Don't bother about the children, Mrs. Parker will love it.' "[14]

Now that Milne is dead, Pooh must stand on his own four paws. Not long ago he was ridiculed by Thomas Meehan in an article called "Not Good Taste, Not Bad Taste—It's Camp," which defines "Camp" as a term to "describe a previously unnamed sensibility, a third stream of taste, entirely apart from good taste or bad taste, that encompasses the curious attraction that everyone—to some degree, at least—has for the bizarre, the unnatural, the artificial and the blatantly outrageous. In short, Camp has come along to fill the singular need for a word to describe all those things that, until recently, have been called 'so bad they're good.'...."Meehan then lists such examples of Camp as Oscar Wilde, art nouveau, Tiffany lamps, Batman comic books, most Joan Crawford movies since *Mildred Pierce*, and *Winnie-the-Pooh*.[15] The inclusion of Pooh in such preposterous company is itself an example of Camp as defined by Meehan: bizarre, unnatural, artificial, and blatantly outrageous. Pooh's fur has not been ruffled. It is only necessary to hurl at his critics the charge which Milne reserved for those who fail to appreciate Kenneth Grahame, that they have sat in judgment on themselves.

What is Pooh's future? To judge by his past and present, it will be forested with bee-trees and opulent with honey pots. The current market for children's books, in spite of its emphasis on the practical and its superabundance of space-age books, swarms with animal fantasies from *Alice in Wonderland* through the *Stuart Little* of E. B. White, the Dr. Seuss stories, and *The Bat Poet* of Randall Jarrell. In the comic strips, Walt Disney has long since raised a large-eared mouse and petulant duck to world renown; Pogo, the possum, has brought politics to the Okefenokee Swamp; and Snoopy of *Peanuts* has furnished his dog house with a Van Gogh and a pool table. There is even a bear named Yogi, famous also on television, a fat, clownish fellow with a hearty appetite, a kind of rustic American cousin to the equally large-tummied but more urbane Pooh.

Winnie-the-Pooh, who doubtless has had a paw in the current vogue for talking animals, seems more than able to hold his part of the forest against their encroachments. He shuffles through the grass, composing a hum or anticipating breakfast. Celebrity? Immortality?—he cannot pronounce such words, much less spell them. He thinks of himself as a Silly Old Bear. But that is part of his charm. He underestimates himself.

Notes and References

Preface

1. *It's Too Late Now: The Autobiography of a Writer* (London, 1939), p. 3.
2. *Ibid.*, p. 211.
3. Grahame Greene, "Letters and the Arts," *Living Age*, CCCXLVI (March, 1934), 78.

Chapter One

1. *By Way of Introduction* (London, 1929), p. 4.
2. *Not That It Matters* (London, 1949), p. 40.
3. *It's Too Late Now*, p. 97.
4. *By Way of Introduction*, p. 193.
5. *Those Were the Days* (London, 1947), p. vii.
6. *Ibid.*, p. v.
7. *Ibid.*, p. 60.
8. Stanley J. Kunitz and Howard Haycraft, *Twentieth-Century Authors* (New York, 1942), p. 965.
9. *Not That It Matters*, pp. 107–8.
10. *Ibid.*, p. 237.
11. *By Way of Introduction*, pp. 58–59.
12. *Ibid.*, p. 27.
13. *Ibid.*, p. 15–16.
14. *Ibid.*, p. 21.
15. *Ibid.*, pp. 203–5.
16. *Peace with Honour* (London, 1934), pp. 179–84.
17. *War with Honour* (London, 1940), p. 12.
18. *War Aims Unlimited* (London, 1949), p. 24.
19. *Year In, Year Out*, illustrated by Ernest Shepard (London, 1952), p. 15.
20. *Ibid.*, p. 71.
21. *Ibid.*, p. 152.
22. *Ibid.*, p. 120.
23. *Ibid.*, p. 100.

Chapter Two

1. *It's Too Late Now*, pp. 244–48.

2. George Jean Nathan, *The World in Falseface* (New York, 1923), pp. 131–32.
3. *Ibid.*, p. 131.
4. *It's Too Late Now*, p. 224.
5. *Year In, Year Out*, p. 121.
6. *Second Plays* (London, 1928), p. xiii.
7. *It's Too Late Now*, p. 235.
8. *It's Too Late Now*, p. x.
9. *Second Plays*, p. 246.
10. *It's Too Late Now*, p. 249.
11. Frank Swinnerton, *The Georgian Scene: A Literary Panorama* (New York, 1934), p. 124.

Chapter Three

1. *The Ivory Door* (London, 1929), pp. v–vi.
2. *Not That It Matters*, p. 89.
3. In *Why Steinbeck Wrote "The Grapes of Wrath" and Other Essays*, by Joseph Henry Jackson *et al.* (New York, 1940), pp. 26–27.
4. Peter Green, *Kenneth Grahame: A Biography* (Cleveland, 1959), p. 347.
5. *Michael and Mary* (London, 1931), p. xx.
6. *Miss Elizabeth Bennet* (London, 1936), p. viii.
7. *Before the Flood* (New York and London, 1951), p. 26.

Chapter Four

1. *Once on a Time* (New York, 1962), p. v.
2. *It's Too Late Now*, p. 213.
3. *Once on a Time*, p. v.
4. *Ibid.*, p. 10.
5. *Ibid.*, p. 103.
6. *Ibid.*, p. 46.
7. *Ibid.*, pp. 126–27.

Chapter Five

1. *When We Were Very Young*, in *Pooh's Library* (New York, 1952), p. 102.
2. *Ibid.*, p. vii.
3. *Ibid.*, p. 101.
4. Annie Moore, *Literature Old and New for Children* (Boston, 1934), p. 239.
5. *When We Were Very Young*, p. 62.
6. *Ibid.*, p. 6.

7. *Ibid.*, p. 43.
8. *Ibid.*, p. 33.
9. In *The Poetical Works* (London, 1924), p. 428.
10. *When We Were Very Young*, p. 30.
11. *The Poetical Works*, p. 428.
12. *Now We Are Six*, in *Pooh's Library* (New York, 1961), p. vi.
13. *Ibid.*, p. 8.
14. *Ibid.*, p. 85.
15. *Ibid.*, p. 97.
16. Eugene Field, *Poems of Childhood* (New York, 1904), p. 66.
17. Mary Hill Arbuthnot, *Children and Books* (Chicago, 1947), p. 94.

Chapter Six

1. *A Gallery of Children* (London, 1939), p. 88.
2. *When We Were Very Young*, p. 87.
3. *Winnie-the-Pooh*, in *Pooh's Library* (New York, 1961), p. 4.
4. *It's Too Late Now*, p. 29.
5. *By Way of Introduction*, p. 26.
6. *Winnie-the-Pooh*, p. 54.
7. *Ibid.*, p. 147.
8. *The House at Pooh Corner*, in *Pooh's Library* (New York, 1961), p. 108.
9. *Ibid.*, p. 57.
10. *Ibid.*, p. 178.

Chapter Seven

1. "Always Time for a Rhyme," *The New York Herald-Tribune Book Review*, XXIX (October 12, 1952), 10.
2. *Year In, Year Out*, p. 71.
3. *Mr. Pim Passes By* (London, 1921), p. 98.
4. *Ibid.*, p. 50.
5. *Ibid.*, p. 113.
6. *The Red House Mystery* (New York, 1936), p. vii.
7. *Ibid.*, pp. viii–x.
8. *Year In, Year Out*, pp. 138–39.
9. Dwight Whitney, "Case of the Indestructible Hero," *TV Guide* (July 4–10, 1964), p. 18.
10. *Chloe Marr* (London, 1946), p. 45.
11. "*Chloe Marr*," XCVIII (September 2, 1946), 98.

Chapter Eight

1. *It's Too Late Now,* p. 119.
2. *"Behind the Lines," The New York Herald-Tribune,* XVII (January 26, 1941), 8.
3. *The Norman Church* (London, 1948), p. 17.
4. *Ibid.,* p. 37.
5. *Birthday Party* (New York, 1948), p. 7.

Chapter Nine

1. *Year In, Year Out,* pp. 137–38.
2. *A Table Near the Band,* p. 146.
3. *Birthday Party,* pp. 228–29.
4. Frank Swinnerton, *The Georgian Scene,* p. 122.
5. *By Way of Introduction,* p. 27.
6. *Ibid.,* pp. 131–32.
7. *It's Too Late Now,* p. 31.
8. Alexander Leonard, *The Valley of the Latin Bear* (New York, 1965), pp. 173–75.
9. *Ibid.,* pp. 180–81.
10. *Ibid.,* p. 217.
11. Frederick C. Crews, *The Pooh Perplex* (New York, 1963), pp. 21–23.
12. *Ibid.,* p. 44.
13. *Ibid.,* p. 75.
14. *It's Too Late Now,* p. 238.
15. Thomas Meehan, "Not Good Taste, Not Bad Taste—It's Camp," *The New York Times Magazine,* CXIV (March 21, 1965), 30–31.

Selected Bibliography

PRIMARY SOURCES

I. Essays

The Ascent of Man. London: Ernest Benn Ltd., 1928.
By Way of Introduction. London: Methuen and Co., 1939.
Going Abroad?. London: Council for Education in World Citizenship, 1947.
If I May. London: Methuen and Co., 1948.
Lovers in London. London: Alston Rivers, 1905.
Not That It Matters. London: Methuen and Co., 1949.
Peace with Honour. London: Methuen and Co., 1934.
Those Were the Days: The Day's Play, The Holiday Round, Once a Week, and The Sunny Side. London: Methuen and Co., 1947.
War Aims Unlimited. London: Methuen and Co., 1941.
War with Honour. London: Macmillan and Co., 1940.
Year In, Year Out. Illustrated by Ernest H. Shepard. London: Methuen and Co., 1952.

II. Plays

The Artist: A Duologue. New York and London: Samuel French, Ltd., 1923.
Before the Flood. New York and London: Samuel French, Ltd., 1951.
First Plays. London: Chatto and Windus, 1928.
Four Plays. London: Chatto and Windus, 1929.
The Ivory Door. London: Chatto and Windus, 1929.
The Man in the Bowler Hat: A Terribly Exciting Affair. New York and London: Samuel French, Ltd., 1923.
Michael and Mary. London: Chatto and Windus, 1931.
Miss Elizabeth Bennet: A Play from Pride and Prejudice. London: Chatto and Windus, 1936.
Miss Marlow at Play. New York and London: Samuel French, Ltd., 1936.
Other People's Lives. New York and London: Samuel French, Ltd., 1932.
The Perfect Alibi: A Detective Story in Three Acts. New York and London: Samuel French, Ltd., 1928.
Sarah Simple. New York and London: Samuel French, Ltd., 1939.

Second Plays. London: Chatto and Windus, 1928.
Three Plays. London: Chatto and Windus, 1929.
Toad of Toad Hall. New York: Charles Scribner's Sons, 1965.
The Ugly Duckling in *Twenty-Four Favorite One-Act Plays*, edited by Bennett Cerf and Van H. Cartmell (New York: Dolphin Books, 1963), 433–55.

III. Juveniles

The Christopher Robin Story Book. New York: E. P. Dutton and Co., 1961.
A Gallery of Children. Illustrated by A. H. Watson. London: George G. Harrap and Co., 1939.
Once on a Time. Illustrated by Susan Perl. New York: New York Graphic Society, 1962.
Pooh's Birthday Book. Illustrated by Ernest H. Shepard. New York: E. P. Dutton and Co., 1963.
Pooh's Library: When We Were Very Young, Winnie-the-Pooh, Now We Are Six, and *The House at Pooh Corner*. Illustrated by Ernest H. Shepard. New York: E. P. Dutton and Co., 1961.
The Pooh Song Book. Illustrated by Ernest H. Shepard. Music by H. Fraser-Simson. New York: E. P. Dutton and Co., 1961.
The Pooh Story Book. Illustrated by Ernest H. Shepard. New York: E. P. Dutton and Co., 1965.

IV. Novels

Chloe Marr. London: Methuen and Co., 1946.
Four Days' Wonder. London: Methuen and Co., 1933.
Mr. Pim Passes By. London: Methuen and Co., 1929.
The Red House Mystery. New York: E. P. Dutton and Co., 1936.
Two People. London: Methuen and Co., 1931.

V. Poems, Short Stories, and Autobiographies

Behind the Lines. New York: E. P.Dutton and Co., 1940.
Birthday Party. New York: E. P. Dutton and Co., 1948.
For the Luncheon Interval. London: Methuen and Co., 1925.
It's Too Late Now: The Autobiography of a writer. London: Methuen and Co., 1939.
The Norman Church. London: Methuen and Co., 1948.
The Secret and Other Stories. New York: The Fountain Press, 1929.
A Table Near the Band. London: Methuen and Co., 1950.
When I Was Very Young. Illustrated by Ernest H. Shepard, New York: The Fountain Press, 1930.

VI. Uncollected Articles and Verses

"Always Time for a Rhyme," *The New York Herald-Tribune Book Review*, XXIX (October 12, 1952), 10.
"Mr. Grahame, Mr. Roosevelt, and I." *Why Steinbeck Wrote 'The Grapes of Wrath' and Other Essays*. New York: Limited Editions Club, 1940.
"Play Writing and Play Selling." *The Writer's Desk Book*. London: A. and C. Black, Ltd., 1934. 70–74.
"This England—According to Milne," *The New York Times Magazine*, XCII (July 25, 1943), 7, 17.

SECONDARY SOURCES

I. A Nutshell Library for Fans of Winnie-the-Pooh.

BARRIE, J. M. *Peter and Wendy*. New York: Charles Scribner's Sons, 1918. Barrie's original story of Peter Pan, from which he adapted his play, and not the story as sentimentalized by various later authors.
BAUM, L. FRANK. *Wizard of Oz* and *Land of Oz*. New York: Random House, 1960. Two classics in a series begun magnificently by Baum but continued after his death *ad infinitum* and *ad nauseam* by Dorothy Plumly Thompson.
BELLOC, HILAIRE. *The Bad Child's Book of Beasts* and *More Beasts for Worse Children* and *A Moral Alphabet*. Illustrated by B.T.B. New York: Dover Publications, Inc., 1961. Good verses, mostly zoological, for bad children; a probable influence on Milne's better verses for better children.
CARROLL, LEWIS. *Alice in Wonderland, Through the Looking-Glass,* and *The Hunting of the Snark*. Illustrated by John Tenniel, with an introduction by Alexander Woollcott. New York: The Modern Library, undated. The great Victorian classics which enlarged the tradition of the beast fable by aiming to amuse instead of to instruct.
DE LA MARE, WALTER. *Peacock Pie*. Illustrated by Barbara Cooney. New York: Alfred A. Knopf, Inc., 1961. Poems about children whom "magic hath stolen away" and other fey beings. Early critics compared *When We Were Very Young* to *Peacock Pie*, though Milne is less fanciful, more practical.
FIELD, EUGENE. *Poems of Childhood*. New York: Charles Scribner's Sons, 1904. Saccharine, if melodious, verses redeemed by "Little Boy Blue" and a handful of other poignancies.
GARIS, HOWARD R. *Uncle Wiggily's Story Book*. New York: Platt and Munk, undated. Badly written but imaginatively plotted stories

with a host of villains—the Woozie Wolf, the Skeezicks, and others—to rival the dreaded Heffalump.

GRAHAME, KENNETH. *The Wind in the Willows*. Illustrated by Ernest H. Shepard. New York: Charles Scribner's Sons, 1961. Along with *Peter Pan*, Milne's favorite book for children, and one which he helped to popularize with two essays and adapted into a play, *Toad of Toad Hall*.

HARRIS, JOEL CHANDLER. *Complete Tales of Uncle Remus*. Edited by Richard Chase. Boston: Houghton, Mifflin and Co., 1955. Old Negro folk tales which Chandler adapted into a children's classic and which Milne's father read aloud to his sons with appropriate dialect.

JARRELL, RANDALL. *The Bat-Poet*. Illustrated by Maurice Sendak. New York: The Macmillan Co., 1964. Prose tale about the most talented and ingratiating beast-poet since Pooh wrote his Hums.

KINGSLEY, Charles. *The Water-Babies: A Fairy Tale for a Land-Baby*. New York: A. L. Burt, Publisher, n.d. A magical if slightly old-fashioned story about water babies, both human and animal.

LOFTING, HUGH. *The Story of Doctor Doolittle*. Philadelphia: J. B. Lippincott Co., 1920. The first and best of the books about the kindly veterinarian who could talk to animals.

POTTER, BEATRIX. *The Tale of Peter Rabbit*. New York: Frederick Warne and Co., n.d. The story in which Miss Potter does for a rabbit what Milne does for a bear.

ROSSETTI, CHRISTINA GEORGINA. *The Poetical Works*. With Memoir and Notes by William Michael Rossetti. London: Macmillan, 1935. Contains the whole of *Sing-Song*, a sweetly naïve collection of verses for children; separate and later editions usually omit the sadder poems.

SCHULZ, C. M. *Peanuts*. New York: Holt, Rinehart and Winston, 1952. First of many hilarious collections featuring the misadventurous Charlie Brown and his canine Pooh, Snoopy.

SEUSS, DR. *The Cat in the Hat*. New York: Random House, 1957. Inspired jingles by a disciple of Milne.

STEVENSON, ROBERT LOUIS. *A Child's Garden of Verses*. Illustrated by Steffie E. Lerch. Chicago: Wilcox and Follett Co., 1948. Verses for children by the great Victorian romancer; light and lilting of melody but content sometimes heavy of moral.

TOLKIEN, J. R. R. *The Hobbit*. Boston: Houghton Mifflin Co., 1938. A lively enchantment in which a famous English scholar invades children's literature to introduce a creature part elf and part rabbit and send him on a perilous search for gold—and Hobbit-hood.

TRAVERS, P. L. *The Mary Poppins Library*. New York: Harcourt, Brace and World, 1952. The original *Mary Poppins* and three other stories about the "practically perfect" governess who travels by umbrella and descends with the suddenness of a hailstorm to champion misunderstood children against stuffy parents.

WHITE, E. B. *Stuart Little.* Illustrated by Garth Williams. New York: Harper and Row, 1945. Whimsicality becomes enduring art in this wise and humorous tale of a mouse who is born to human parents.

WHITE, T. H. *The Sword and the Stone.* New York: G. P. Putnam's Sons, White's Medieval classic about King Arthur as a boy; the prelude to the books which inspired the Broadway musical, *Camelot.*

II. Works about Milne and His Era

ARBUTHNOT, MAY HILL. *Children and Books.* Chicago: Scott, Foresman and Co., 1947. Judicious evaluation of Milne's gifts as a poet for children, with an honest look at his deficiencies in "lyric beauty" and "delicate imagery."

BARRIE, J. M. *Letters.* Edited by Viola Meynell. New York: Charles Scribner's Sons, 1947. Contains four letters from Barrie to Milne, the first of which praises *The Day's Play* and begins the long friendship between the two men; the last of which congratulates Milne on the birth of Christopher Robin.

"Behind the Lines." *The New York Herald-Tribune Books,* XVII (January 26, 1941), 8. A review which grants sincerity but doubts distinction in Milne's poems inspired by World War II.

BLUM, DANIEL. *A Pictorial History of the American Theatre: 1860–1960.* New York: Bonanza Books (Crown Publishers, Inc.), 1960. Mediocre in text, magnificent in pictures, this record of the American theater shows the original Broadway casts of *Mr. Pim Passes By, The Dover Road,* and other Milne favorites of the Twenties.

"Chloe Marr." *Time,* XCVIII (September 2, 1946), 98. A review and a condemnation of Milne's last novel: "Pooh is the word for *Chloe Marr.*"

CREWS, FREDERICK C. *The Pooh Perplex.* New York: E. P. Dutton and Co., Inc., 1963. Clever parody of modern criticism, in which Winnie-the-Pooh triumphs over assorted critics, from Marxists to Angry Young Men.

DOWNEY, FAIRFAX. *When We Were Rather Older.* Illustrated by Jefferson Machamer. New York: Minton, Balch, and Co., 1926. Strained, tedious parody of *When We Were Very Young,* with flappers and college blades instead of Christopher Robin and his Nanny.

DUKES, ASHLEY. *The Youngest Drama: Studies of Fifty Dramatists.* Chicago: Charles H. Sergel and Co., 1924. Critique of Milne in his early days as a dramatist, with special attention to *The Dover Road* and *The Truth about Blayds.*

ERSKINE, JOHN. *The Private Life of Helen of Troy.* New York: The Sun Dial Press, 1942. Intimate and impudent view of the face that launched a thousand ships; one of the books which Milne would most have liked to write and an obvious influence on his play about Noah, *Before the Flood.*

GREEN, PETER. *Kenneth Grahame: A Biography.* Cleveland and New York: World Publishing Co., 1959. Definitive biography of Grahame which treats his friendship with Milne but unfairly dismisses Milne's adaptation of *Wind in the Willows* as mawkish and sentimental.

HARTOG, JAN DE. *The Distant Shore.* New York: Harper and Brothers, 1951. Novel in which Christopher Robin makes an unlikely but welcome appearance aboard a Dutch tugboat during World War II.

HIGHET, GILBERT. "Poor Winnie in Pooh-Latin," *Horizon,* III (July, 1961), 112–15. Surprisingly virulent attack on Alexander Leonard's *Winnie ille Pu,* which Highet condemns as a "trifling book" in ponderous Latin, "full of awkward mistakes."

HOLDEN, SUZANNE. "Fashion Explores the World of Pooh," *The Norfolk Ledger-Star* (July 9, 1965), p. 8. Illustrated article about the Winnie-the-Pooh fashions introduced by Sears Roebuck for the very young.

KUNITZ, STANLEY AND HAYCRAFT, HOWARD. *Twentieth Century Authors.* New York: H. W. Wilson Co., 1942. Delightful if none too accurate sketch of Milne, with a fair estimate of his weakness for "milk-and-water" whimsicality and a fair appraisal of his "genuinely witty and satirical talent."

LEONARD, ALEXANDER. *The Valley of the Latin Bear.* Foreword by Robert Graves. New York: E. P. Dutton and Co., 1965. Rambling but piquant autobiography by the Hungarian doctor who translated *Winnie-the-Pooh* into Latin and startled the publishing world when his translation became a phenomenal seller.

"Letters and the Arts," *Living Age,* CCCXLVI (March, 1934), 78. Amusing account of a feud between Milne and Grahame Greene, in which Greene insisted that Milne was not a humorist but a "cheer leader in a great community laugh," and in which Milne replied that Greene harbored sex repressions.

LIFKA, M. "Pooh to you!," *Catholic World,* CLXXXIV (December, 1956), 185–89. Memorial to Milne in the form of thumbnail sketches of his famous animals with emphasis on Pooh and Eeyore and with appropriate quotations from Milne himself.

MACKAIL, DENIS. *Barrie: The Story of J.M.B.* New York: Charles
    Scribner's Sons, 1941. Excellent treatment of the theatrical world
    of the 1910's into which Barrie introduced Milne when he spon-
    sored *Wurzel-Flummery.*
"A Man Who Hated Whimsy," *Time*, LXVII (February 13, 1956),
    56. Affectionate obituary of Milne by a magazine not always kind
    to his books.
MEEHAN, THOMAS. "Not Good Taste, Not Bad Taste—It's 'Camp,' "
    The New York Times Magazine, CXIV (March 21, 1965), 30–31,
    113–15. Article lumps *Winnie-the-Pooh* with Batman comic books
    and Tiffany Lamps and brands it as "Camp"—that is, so bad that
    it seems good.
MOORE, ANNE CARROLL. *The Three Owls: A Book about Children's
    Books.* New York: Macmillan Co., 1925. Commendation of Milne
    for catching "the very music of childhood" in his Christopher
    Robin poems.
MOORE, ANNIE E. *Literature Old and New for Children.* Boston:
    Houghton Mifflin Co., 1934. Biographical sketch of Milne and a
    graceful appreciation of his children's books for capturing
    "whimsy and ideality and realism."
NATHAN, GEORGE JEAN. *The World in Falseface.* New York: Alfred
    A. Knopf, Inc., 1923. Observations and criticisms by the one-time
    dean of the American theater, with a harsh but accurate estimate
    of Milne as one of the "lesser British dramatists."
SWINNERTON, FRANK. *The Georgian Scene: A Literary Panorama.* New
    York: Farrar and Rinehart, 1934. Penetrating account of Milne
    as a man and a writer, with praise for his gentleness, reproof for
    his placidness.
WELLS, H. G. *Experiment in Autobiography: Discoveries and Conclu-
    sions of a Very Ordinary Brain.* New York: Macmillan Co., 1934.
    Autobiography of a famous writer who attended school at Henley
    House, which was run by Milne's father, whom Wells thought
    "a really able teacher." He mentions A. A.'s first appearance in
    print at the age of six in *The Henley House Magazine.*
WHITNEY, DWIGHT. "Case of the Indestructible Hero," *TV Guide*
    (July 4–10, 1964), pp. 15–19. Interview with Erle Stanley Gard-
    ner which, though Milne is never mentioned, highlights the cur-
    rent tendency of mystery writers to create faceless, shadowy
    heroes, in contrast to the meticulously characterized hero of *The
    Red House Mystery.*
"Winnie-the-Pooh Tours U.S.," *Life*, XXX (February 19, 1951),
    75–76, 79. Pictorial account of an American tour made by the
    stuffed originals of Pooh, Piglet, Eeyore, Kanga, and Tigger,
    which are now lodged in the New York offices of E. P. Dutton

and Co. Christopher Robin is shown at the age of six with his father and Pooh, and again in 1948 with his new bride.

"World of Pooh Lives On," *Life Magazine*, XL (February 27, 1956), 115–20, 122. Pictorial record of Christopher Robin from two through thirty-five, with pictures of his toy animals and of the forgotten penguin which somehow never got into the four famous juveniles.

"Year In, Year Out." The New York Herald-Tribune Book Review, XXIX (November 16, 1952), 5. Review of Milne's last book and a good summary of his best work in all fields: "He has perfect vision out of a small window. . . ."

Index

82570

828.912
Sw972

82570

DATE DUE

GAYLORD			PRINTED IN U.S.A.